London

HarperCollins*Publishers*

Windsor

YOUR COLLINS TRAVELLER

Your Collins Traveller Guide will help you find your way around your chosen destination quickly and easily. It is colour-coded for easy reference:

The blue section answers the question 'I would like to see or do something; where do I go and what do I see when I get there?' This section is arranged as an alphabetical list of topics. Within each topic you will find:
- A selection of the best examples on offer.
- How to get there, costs and opening hours for each entry.
- The outstanding features of each entry.
- A simplified map, with each entry plotted and the nearest landmark or transport access.

The red section is a lively and informative gazetteer. It offers:
- Essential facts about the main places and cultural items.
  What is La Bastille? Who was Michelangelo? Where is Delphi?

The gold section is full of practical and invaluable travel information. It offers:
- Everything you need to know to help you enjoy yourself and get the most out of your time away, from Accommodation through Baby-sitters, Car Hire, Food, Health, Money, Newspapers, Taxis, Telephones to Youth Hostels.

Cross-references:

Type in small capitals – **CHURCHES** – tells you that more information on an item is available within the topic on churches.

A-Z after an item tells you that more information is available within the gazetteer. Simply look under the appropriate name.

A name in bold – **Holy Cathedral** – also tells you that more information on an item is available in the gazetteer – again simply look up the name.

CONTENTS

CONTENTS

■ PRACTICAL INFORMATION GAZETTEER

INTRODUCTION

Attached to the downstream side of Charing Cross railway bridge is a narrow and fragile-seeming walkway, known as the Hungerford Footbridge, which enables pedestrians to cross the Thames between Victoria Embankment and the South Bank. Go on to the walkway not too late on a fine night, stop halfway across to gaze downriver (ignoring as best you can the shivering of the ground beneath your feet as trains clank by behind you) and you will be rewarded with a view as magnificent as any city in the world can offer and one that seems peculiarly to encapsulate the special qualities and attractions of London.

Here the Thames, as though gathering itself for its final surge into the sea 50 miles on, alters course from northwards to eastwards, shrinking your view of its south bank but disclosing its north bank in a long, concave swathe. And in the light-studded panorama laid out before you, past and present splendidly coexist, London's successive historical personas proving as powerful a presence as its vibrant contemporary self. To your right you have the undilutedly modern, and at night very impressive, spectacle of the South Bank Centre – the glass river frontage of the Royal Festival Hall ablaze with light, the shadowy geometric shapes of the Queen Elizabeth Hall and the Hayward Gallery further on, with the London Weekend Television tower block rearing up, busily bright beyond. To your left and ahead of you, curving round with the river to the limit of your vision, is a much more complex cityscape, rich with architectural variety. Distant high-rise buildings – Telecom Tower, Centrepoint, the Barbican towers, the NatWest tower – glow against the night sky, all proclaiming London to be a city of the late 20thC. Yet nearer at hand (or made to seem so by floodlighting) are landmarks of a different ilk and other styles: Shell-Mex House from the 1930s, Somerset House from the late 18thC, the early-18thC steeple of St. Bride's and the 17thC St. Paul's all portray another London – a city which has grown decade by decade and century by century. The two notions are not incompatible. London has always readily renewed itself but never so as to wipe out all trace of the old. Each period of the city's history – Roman, Saxon, Norman, Medieval, Tudor, Elizabethan, Stuart, Georgian, Regency and Victorian – is to some degree still manifest alongside the constructions of the 20thC. For resident and visitor alike, this is a source of curiosity and a gratification, as well as an unfailing

pleasure. If, from your vantage point of Hungerford Footbridge, you look beyond Waterloo Bridge to the north side of the Thames, you will see where London began its existence. In AD 43 the legions of Claudius established on the raised ground of Cornhill a settlement which they were to call Londinium. Eighty years later the settlement had spread to neighbouring Ludgate Hill and become the largest city in the British Isles. Not until the 11thC, after many vicissitudes, did London replace Winchester as the capital of England, but thereafter its status was secure. By the 19thC the one-time outpost of the Roman Empire had become the hub of the British Empire, and although that glory has departed, London remains the mother city of the British Commonwealth.

Just as you can use this historical or temporal approach as your means of getting to know and enjoy London, so there are myriad other ways of extracting enjoyment from the metropolis. A regional approach will allow you to focus on the attractions of particular districts, such as Docklands, the City of London, Soho, Westminster, Greenwich, Chelsea or Highgate. Or you may wish to concentrate on the famous buildings which are scattered so liberally throughout the capital, such as St. Paul's, the Tower, Greenwich Hospital, Westminster Abbey and Buckingham Palace. Alternatively you may want to test the city's reputation as a mecca for shoppers by investigating for yourself such venues as Oxford St, Bond St, Burlington Arcade, Jermyn St, Knightsbridge and the King's Rd or, for a more raffish style, the ambience of a market like Portobello Rd, Camden Lock, Petticoat Lane or Bermondsey. Should you find that the crowds are proving a strain, you can gain respite in one of the many parks in the capital, such as Hyde Park, where you can go for a row, practise your putting on the greens or listen to a concert. Refreshed, you may feel ready to visit a museum – perhaps the world-famous British Museum or the Victoria and Albert. And if you are an art-lover you mustn't miss the National Gallery, the Tate or the Whitechapel.

A perfect way to spend the evening may be in the pursuit of culture or just sheer enjoyment – a visit to the opera or to a concert, to a performance at Covent Garden or to a recital at the Queen Elizabeth Hall. The theatre, too, offers so much, from the musicals and comedies on

Shaftesbury Ave to Shakespearian tragedies at the Barbican. Finally, if your taste is for ceremony and tradition, you will find plenty to please, and you should try to witness at least one of the following events: the Ceremony of the Keys at the Tower of London, the Changing of the Guard at Buckingham Palace, Trooping the Colour, the State Opening of Parliament, the Lord Mayor's Procession – and Doggett's Coat and Badge Race on the Thames. When all is considered, you may decide that seldom has a pronouncement, thrown off in a letter, stood the test of time so well as Johnson's observation to Boswell that 'there is in London all that life can afford'.

And on a fine night you may decide to walk across Hungerford Foot-bridge with nothing more definite in mind than to look at the view and watch the Thames slip away from you. London provides for every mood.

Hampton Court

HAMPTON COURT PALACE

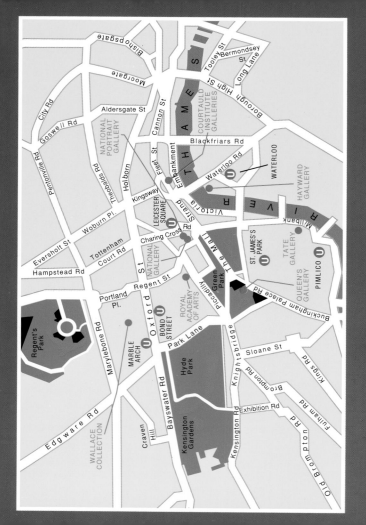

NATIONAL GALLERY Trafalgar Sq., WC2.
■ 1000-1800 Mon.-Sat., 1400-1800 Sun. BR/U Charing Cross. ● Free.
Tours. Disabled.
Unrivalled display of western European artistic masterpieces. See **A-Z**.

TATE GALLERY Millbank, SW1.
■ 1000-1750 Mon.-Sat., 1400-1750 Sun. U Pimlico. ● Free. Disabled.
16th-20thC British art. The Clore Gallery is devoted to Turner. See **A-Z**.

ROYAL ACADEMY OF ARTS Burlington House, Piccadilly, W1.
■ 1000-1800. U Piccadilly Circus. ● £3-5. Disabled.
Holds the famous annual summer exhibition of contemporary artists.

COURTAULD INSTITUTE GALLERIES Somerset House, The
Strand, WC2. ■ 1000-1700 Mon.-Sat., 1400-1800 Sun. U Temple (Sun.
Embankment). ● £3, OAP/child 5-18 £1.50. Disabled.
Splendid French impressionists and postimpressionists. See **WALK 2**, **A-Z**.

NATIONAL PORTRAIT GALLERY St. Martin's Pl., WC2.
■ 1000-1700 Mon.-Fri., 1000-1800 Sat., 1400-1800 Sun.
BR/U Charing Cross. ● Free.
See the famous and the infamous. Excellent photograph collection.

QUEEN'S GALLERY Buckingham Palace Rd, SW1.
■ 1000-1700 Tue.-Sat., 1400-1700 Sun. U Victoria, St. James's Park.
● £2, OAP £1.50, child 5-16 £1.
Paintings and art treasures from the royal collections. See **WALK 1**.

HAYWARD GALLERY South Bank Centre, SE1.
■ 1000-1800 Thu.-Mon., 1000-2000 Tue. & Wed. BR/U Waterloo.
● £5. Disabled.
Temporary exhibitions of historical and contemporary fine art.

WALLACE COLLECTION Hertford House, Manchester Sq., W1.
■ 1000-1700 Mon.-Sat., 1400-1700 Sun. U Bond St. ● Free. Disabled.
Impressive collection including 17th-18thC French paintings, sculpture.

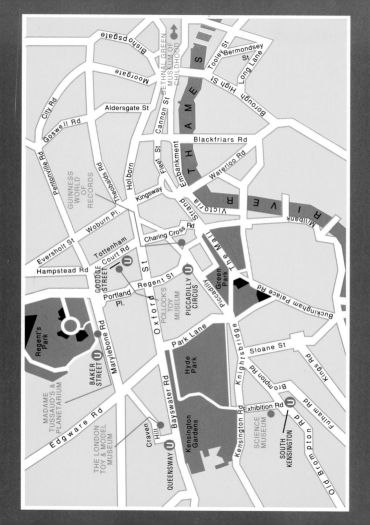

SCIENCE MUSEUM Exhibition Rd, SW7.

■ 1000-1800 Mon.-Sat., 1100-1800 Sun. U South Kensington.
● £3.50, OAP £2, child 5-15 £1.75, family (2+4) £15. Disabled.
The Children's Gallery is very popular. Youngsters can examine a number of scientific displays and models. Don't forget to see the steam locomotives and early aircraft too. See **A-Z**.

GUINNESS WORLD OF RECORDS Piccadilly Circus, W1.
■ 1000-2200. U Piccadilly Circus. ● £5, OAP £3.95, child 5-15 £3.20. Disabled.
The world of superlatives, with life-size exhibits, models and videos.

POLLOCK'S TOY MUSEUM 1 Scala St, W1.
■ 1000-1700 Mon.-Sat. U Goodge St. ● £1.50, child 3-18 50p.
A delightful collection of antique toys, dolls and games in an old house.

MADAME TUSSAUD'S & PLANETARIUM Marylebone Rd, NW1. ■ 0900-1730 July & Aug.; 1000-1730 Mon.-Fri., 0930-1730 Sat. & Sun., Sep.-June. U Baker St. ● Madame Tussaud's £5.95, OAP £4.55, child 5-15 £3.95, family (2+2) £15.85. ● Madame Tussaud's & Planetarium £7.75, OAP £6.10, child 5-15 £5.10, family (2+2) £20.60. Disabled.
Enjoy the Chamber of Horrors, historical tableaux and famous personalities of the wax museum, plus the Planetarium's journey into space.

BETHNAL GREEN MUSEUM OF CHILDHOOD
Cambridge Heath Rd, Bethnal Green, E2. ■ 1000-1750 Mon.-Thu. & Sat., 1430-1750 Sun. U Bethnal Green. ● Free.
An extensive collection, including children's toys, games, books and clothes.

THE LONDON TOY & MODEL MUSEUM Craven Hill, W2.
■ 1000-1730 Mon.-Sat., 1100-1730 Sun. & BH. U Queensway.
● £2.80, OAP £1.80, child 5-15 £1.30, family (2+2) £6.40. Disabled.
The history of toys through the ages. You can also travel on a miniature steam train (Sun. only).

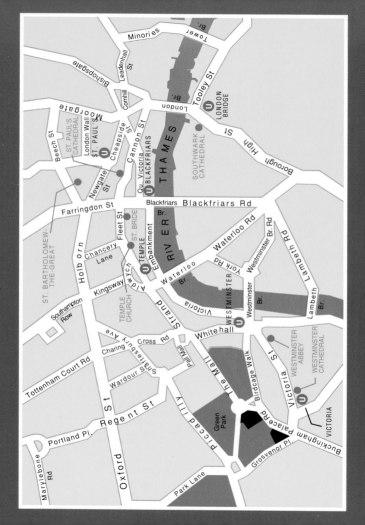

CHURCHES

ST. PAUL'S CATHEDRAL Ludgate Hill, EC4.
■ 0730-1800. U St. Paul's. ● Donation; £1 suggested. Disabled (1+2 steps to lift).
*Wren's (see **A-Z**) greatest work. An architectural masterpiece, from the stunning painted dome to the memorials in the crypt. See **SIGHTSEEING 2**.*

WESTMINSTER ABBEY Broad Sanctuary, SW1.
■ Nave 0800-1800 Mon.-Sat. (until 2045 Wed.); according to services Sun. U Westminster. ● Royal Chapels £3, OAP £1.50, child 5-15 £1 (all free 1800-1945 Wed.). For other sections, see **A-Z**. Disabled.
*Superb Gothic structure. Site of royal coronations since 1066. See **A-Z**.*

WESTMINSTER CATHEDRAL Ashley Pl., SW1.
■ 0700-2000. BR/U Victoria. ● Tower lift 70p, OAP/child 40p. Disabled.
Catholic cathedral built in 1903 in the Byzantine style, with an ornate marble and mosaic interior.

ST. BARTHOLOMEW-THE-GREAT West Smithfield, EC1.
■ 0800-1600 Mon.-Sat., 0800-2000 Sun. U St. Paul's. Disabled.
London's oldest parish church, founded in 1123 and restored in 1860s.

ST. BRIDE Fleet St, EC4.
■ 0815-1730. Museum 0900-1700. U Blackfriars. Disabled.
Wren's famous 'wedding cake' steeple. The museum in the crypt reflects the history of Fleet St and the church's role as the 'printers' church'.

SOUTHWARK CATHEDRAL Borough High St, SE1.
■ 0800-1800. U London Bridge.
*One of London's most impressive medieval buildings. See **WALK 3**.*

TEMPLE CHURCH Inner Temple, EC4.
■ 1000-1600 Mon.-Sat., 1300-1600 Sun. U Temple (Sun. Embankment). Disabled.
*Beautiful small round church, built between 1170 and 1240 by the Knights Templar. See **Inns of Court**.*

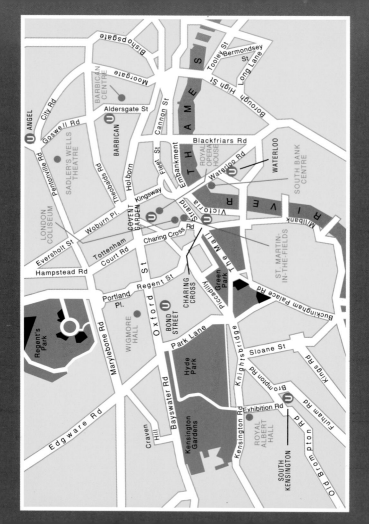

SOUTH BANK CENTRE South Bank, SE1.
BR/U Waterloo. Disabled.
*Visit Royal Festival Hall to hear orchestral and choral concerts, Queen
Elizabeth Hall for chamber music and the Purcell Room for solo recitals.*

ROYAL ALBERT HALL Kensington Gore, SW7, tel: 071-5898212.
U South Kensington.
*Superb Victorian concert hall, best known as the home of the Sir Henry
Wood Promenade Concerts (the Proms; see **Events**).*

BARBICAN CENTRE Silk St, EC2, tel: 071-6384141.
U Barbican (Sun. Moorgate). Disabled.
*Home of London Symphony and English Chamber orchestras. See **A-Z**.*

ROYAL OPERA HOUSE Bow St, WC2, tel: 071-2401066.
Box office in Floral St. U Covent Garden. Disabled.
Home of the world-famous Royal Opera and Royal Ballet companies.

LONDON COLISEUM St. Martin's Lane, WC2, tel: 071-8363161.
U Charing Cross, Leicester Sq.
*The largest auditorium in London. The Coliseum is home to the English
National Opera, and international dance troupes also visit in summer.*

WIGMORE HALL 36 Wigmore St, W1, tel: 071-9352141.
U Oxford Circus, Bond St.
This famous concert hall features recitals and chamber music.

SADLER'S WELLS THEATRE Rosebery Ave, EC1,
tel: 071-2788916. U Angel.
*The most popular dance theatre in London, though no longer home to
Sadler's Wells Royal Ballet.*

ST. MARTIN-IN-THE-FIELDS Trafalgar Sq., WC2,
tel: 071-9300089. U Charing Cross.
*Lovely church famed for its lunchtime chamber- and choral-music
concerts.*

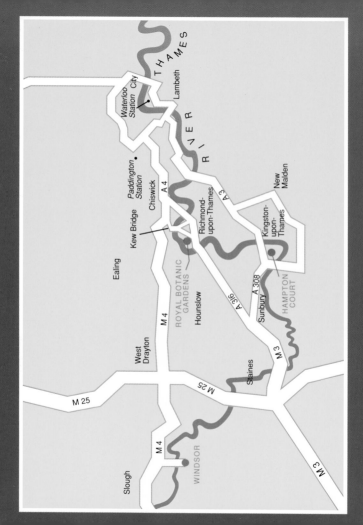

West

Try to allow a full day for your visit to each place.

Royal Botanic Gardens, Kew – 7 miles west of central London.
U Kew Gardens/BR Waterloo to Kew Bridge. ■ Gardens 0930-dusk.
Greenhouses, museum and gallery close 30 min before gardens.
● £3, OAP £1.50, child 5-16 £1. Disabled.
Plant varieties from all over the world are studied at this scientific institution. The grounds contain the superb Palm House, a huge tropical
greenhouse (built in 1844), and the 17thC Kew Palace (1100-1730
April-mid Oct.), the summer home of King George III. The Orangery
(1861) houses temporary exhibitions. See **PARKS**.

Hampton Court – 15 miles southwest of central London. BR Waterloo
to Hampton Court. ■ 0930-1800 summer, 0930-1630 winter. ● £4,
OAP £3, child 5-16 £2.50, family (2+3, 1+4) £12. Disabled.
Built in the early 1500s for Henry VIII's Lord Chancellor, Cardinal
Wolsey, the palace was the apotheosis of Tudor style. It was subsequent-
ly modified by Wren (see **A-Z**) in the early 1700s. No monarch since
George II has lived here. A tour should include the Clock Court, State
apartments, Great Hall and the lovely Fountain Court. The grounds
contain the famous Hampton Court Maze.

Windsor – 21 miles west of central London. BR Paddington to Windsor
Riverside/BR Waterloo to Windsor Central.
Windsor Castle is the royal family's main residence outside London and
is one of the oldest and largest lived-in castles in the world (precincts
open daily; free. Interiors 1100-1300, 1400-1600; £2.80, OAP £1.80,
child 5-16 £1.20). Visit the State apartments, with their collection of
drawings by Michelangelo, Rembrandt and Leonardo, and admire the
beautiful Gothic Chapel of St. George. Nearby in Windsor Great Park is
Savill Gardens (1000-1800 Mar.-Nov.; £2.20, OAP £2, child under 16
free). See also Madame Tussaud's Royalty & Empire exhibition, Windsor
station (0930-1730 summer, 0930-1630 winter; £3.95, OAP £2.95,
child 5-15 £2.80). Across the river is Eton and its famous college.
Founded in 1450 by Henry VI, the school is open to visitors at certain
times; contact Windsor tourist information centre, tel: 0753-852010.

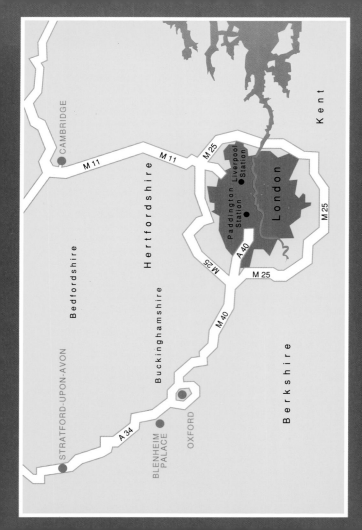

EXCURSIONS 2

North

*To get the most from your trip, allow a day for each place. See also
Collins Traveller: Oxford/Stratford.*

Oxford – 56 miles northwest of London. BR Paddington to Oxford (90
min). By car A 40 and M 40 (90 min-2 hr). Drivers should park on the
outskirts of the town as the centre is largely pedestrianized. Tourist
information centre: St. Aldate's, tel: 0865-726871.
This ancient university town possesses a unique atmosphere,
combining respect for tradition and learning, enshrined in its rich
architectural heritage, with the youthful high spirits of student life. The
Ashmolean Museum in Beaumont St is one of the best provincial
museums in Britain and contains archaeological relics, medieval art
treasures, a rich collection of silverware and drawings by Michelangelo
and Raphael. Visit High St and Broad St, both lined with superb
buildings, and of the colleges try to see New (which is in fact one of the
oldest, dating from 1379), Magdalen, Merton and Christ Church. Go to
the tourist information centre for details of guided tours around the
university buildings and the magnificent Bodleian Library.

Blenheim Palace, Woodstock – 8 miles northwest of Oxford. Bus from
Cornmarket, Oxford. Park 0900-1645 (last entry); 70p, child 5-15 40p.
Palace 1030-1645 (last entry) Mar.-Oct.; £5.50, OAP £4.20, child 5-15
£2.80 (prices include entry to park).
This magnificent palace, part country house, part national monument
and part citadel, was built 1705-22 for John Churchill, the first Duke of
Marlborough, in recognition of his great victory over the French at the
Battle of Blenheim in 1704. His descendent, Winston, was born at
Blenheim in 1874. A guided tour takes you through the striking Great
Hall, the Churchill Exhibition, the lavish State rooms, the outstanding
Long Library with its 10,000 volumes and the chapel with its pompous
tombs fit for royalty. The gardens, too, are superb and extensive. You
will need a full day to see Blenheim, taking in the charming market
town of Woodstock and Churchill's grave, 2 miles south at Bladon.

Stratford-upon-Avon – 97 miles northwest of London, 41 miles north of
Oxford. BR Euston to Coventry, then local bus (2 hr). By car A 40 and

27

Anne Hathaway's Cottage

M 40 to Oxford, then A 34 (2 hr-2 hr 30 min).
Most travel agents can arrange bookings for
organized coach tours from London. Tourist
information centre: Bridge Foot, tel: 0789-293127.
The Shakespearean Properties are a 'must'. Visit
the Bard's house to see the room where he was
born in April 1564, New Place, where he died
aged 52, and Holy Trinity Church to pay respect to
his grave. One-and-a-half miles west of Stratford is
the cottage where Anne Hathaway, Shakespeare's
wife, was born and lived until her marriage, and at
Wilmcote, 3.5 miles north of Stratford, is the house
of his mother, Mary Arden. Stay the night and take
in a performance by the Royal Shakespeare
Company at the Royal Shakespeare Theatre,
located on Waterside. For further information and
reservations, tel: 0789-295623.

Cambridge – 54 miles northeast of London.
BR Liverpool St to Cambridge (75 min). By car
M 11 (90 min). Tourist information centre: Wheeler
St, tel: 0223-322640.
Cambridge is world-famous for its colleges, which
exhibit a wealth of architectural features. Many of
them are open to the public and among the most
notable are Peterhouse, the oldest, which dates
from 1281, Emmanuel and Pembroke with their
chapels designed by Wren (see **A-Z**), and the
superb Gothic perpendicular chapel of King's
College which contains Rubens' *Adoration of the
Magi*. Be sure to see Trinity, the largest college in
Cambridge, and Queen's, with its bridge over the
River Cam. And finally, don't miss the Fitzwilliam
Museum in Trumpington St (1000-1700 Tue.-Sat.,
1415-1700 Sun.; free) which contains an
impressive art collection.

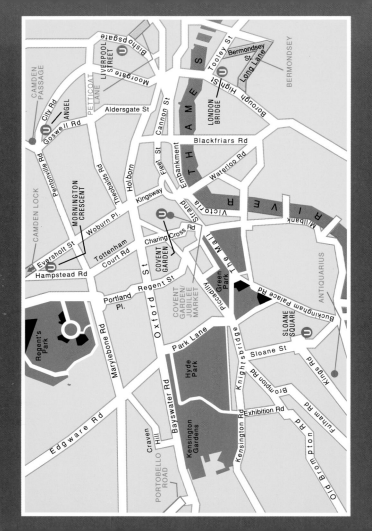

PORTOBELLO ROAD W11.

■ 0800-1500 Fri. (general), 0800-1700 Sat. (antiques). U Notting Hill Gate, Ladbroke Grove.
Famous flea market which is good for antiques, memorabilia, clothes, records and books.

CAMDEN PASSAGE Off Upper St, N1.

■ 0830-1500 Wed. & Sat. U Angel.
Over 350 antiques, jewellery and silver dealers have stalls here twice a week. Permanent shops deal in silver, china, jewellery and collectables.

CAMDEN LOCK Camden High St, NW1.

■ 0800-1800 Sat. & Sun. U Camden Town.
The most fashionable weekend market for crafts, bric-a-brac, antiques and jewellery. The main market is adjacent to Regent's Canal.

PETTICOAT LANE Middlesex St, E1.

■ 0700-1400 Sun. U Liverpool St, Aldgate East.
A typical East End Sun. market which tends to become very crowded after 1100. See also the adjacent Brick Lane – it's cheap and full of character.

BERMONDSEY Long Lane and Bermondsey St, SE1.

■ 0500-1200 Fri. BR/U London Bridge.
Europe's largest antique market includes glass, silver, brassware, maps and prints.

COVENT GARDEN/JUBILEE MARKET WC2.

■ 0700-1700 Mon., 0900-1700 Tue.-Sun. U Covent Garden.
*Mon. for antiques, rest of the week for crafts. Clothes, records and household goods Sun. See **Covent Garden**.*

ANTIQUARIUS 135 King's Rd, SW3.

■ 1000-1800 Mon.-Sat. U Sloane Sq.
Covered antique market with over 200 dealers selling antiques, costume jewellery, china, glass and unusual fashions.

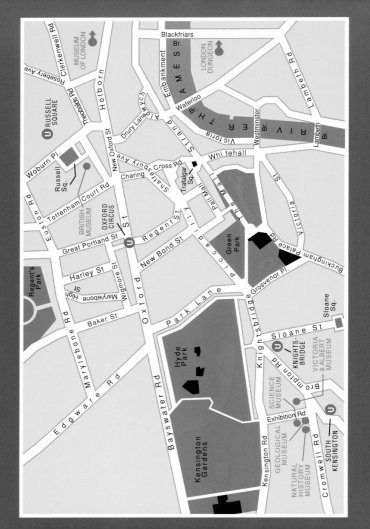

BRITISH MUSEUM Great Russell St, WC1.

▦ 1000-1700 Mon.-Sat., 1430-1830 Sun. Ⓤ Russell Sq., Tottenham Court Road. ● Free. Disabled.

Wonderful collection covering an extensive range of cultures and subjects. See **A-Z.**

VICTORIA & ALBERT MUSEUM Cromwell Rd, SW7.

▦ 1000-1750 Mon.-Sat., 1430-1750 Sun. Ⓤ South Kensington. ● Free; suggested donation £3, OAP/child 5-11 50p.

Possibly the world's greatest applied-art and design collection. See **A-Z.**

SCIENCE MUSEUM Exhibition Rd, SW7.

▦ 1000-1800 Mon.-Sat., 1100-1800 Sun. Ⓤ South Kensington. ● £3.50, OAP £2, child 5-15 £1.75, family (2+4) £15. Disabled.

Excellent coverage of scientific discoveries and applications. See **A-Z.**

NATURAL HISTORY MUSEUM & GEOLOGICAL MUSEUM Cromwell Rd, SW7.

▦ 1000-1800 Mon.-Sat., 1300-1800 Sun. Ⓤ South Kensington. ● £3.50, OAP/child 5-15 £1.55, free 1630-1800 Mon.-Fri., 1700-1800 Sat., Sun. & BH. Disabled.

One of the world's greatest natural-history institutions. The fine Romanesque building, constructed 1873-80, houses fascinating zoology, mineralogy, botany, palaeontology and entomology departments. Note that the museum gets crowded with schoolchildren during term time.

LONDON DUNGEON 28-34 Tooley St, SE1.

▦ 1000-1830 April-Sep., 1000-1730 Oct.-Mar. Ⓤ London Bridge. ● £5, OAP/child 5-14 £3. Disabled.

Vivid depictions of the gruesome methods of torture and execution used in medieval England. Suitable only for older children. See **WALK 3.**

MUSEUM OF LONDON London Wall, EC2.

▦ 1000-1800 Tue.-Sat., 1400-1800 Sun. Ⓤ St. Paul's. ● Free. Disabled.

Portrays the daily life of the city through the ages. Exhibits include historical street scenes. See **A-Z.**

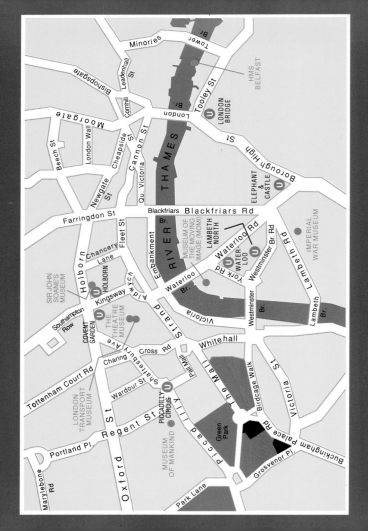

LONDON TRANSPORT MUSEUM 39 Wellington St, Covent
Garden, WC2. ■ 1000-1800. U Covent Garden. ● £3, child 5-16
£1.50, family (2+2) £7. Disabled.
Trains, trams and buses from past to present. See **WALK 2**.

THE THEATRE MUSEUM 1e Tavistock St, Covent Garden, WC2.
■ 1100-1900 Tue.-Sun. U Covent Garden. ● £2.50, child 5-14 £1.50,
family (2+4) £7. Disabled.
The national museum of the performing arts.

MUSEUM OF THE MOVING IMAGE (MOMI)
South Bank Centre, Waterloo, SE1. ■ 1000-2000 June-Sep.; 1000-2000
Mon.-Sat., 1000-1800 Sun. (Oct.-May). U Waterloo. ● £5.50, child
5-16 £4, family (2+4) £16. Disabled.
Intriguing exhibits illustrate the history of television and the cinema.

SIR JOHN SOANE'S MUSEUM 13 Lincoln's Inn Fields, WC2.
■ 1000-1700 Tue.-Sat. Guided tour 1430 Sat. U Holborn. ● Free.
*The splendid art and antiquities collection of 19thC architect John Soane
(see* **Dulwich***).*

IMPERIAL WAR MUSEUM Lambeth Rd, SE1.
■ 1000-1800. U Lambeth North, Elephant & Castle. ● Free Fri. All
other days £3.30, OAP/child 5-16 £1.65. Disabled.
Superb multisensory exhibits cover all aspects of 20thC warfare. See **A-Z**.

HMS BELFAST Morgan's Lane, Tooley St, SE1.
■ 1000-1800 April-Oct., 1000-1630 Nov.-Mar. U London Bridge.
Access via Hay's Galleria or by motor launch from Tower Pier.
● £3.60, child 5-16 £1.80, family (2+2) £9.25.
*One of the largest Royal Navy cruisers ever built, now a floating
museum. Children love it! See* **WALK 3**.

MUSEUM OF MANKIND Burlington Gardens, W1. ■ 1000-1700
Mon.-Sat., 1430-1800 Sun. U Piccadilly Circus. ● Free. Disabled.
Sculptures, pottery, masks and artefacts from different cultures.

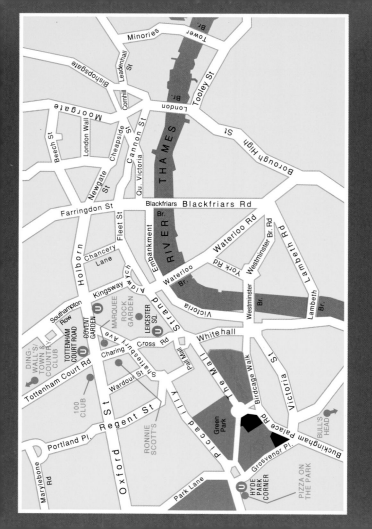

100 CLUB 100 Oxford St, W1.
▪ 1945-0100 Mon.-Sat., 1945-2330 Sun. U Tottenham Ct Rd. ● £3-6.
Jazz club featuring big names in traditional and modern jazz, plus blues and rockabilly.

RONNIE SCOTT'S 47 Frith St, W1.
▪▪ 2030-0300 Mon.-Sat., 2000-2330 Sun. U Leicester Sq. ● £10-12.
London's jazz mecca. Rock, soul and world music on Sun.

PIZZA ON THE PARK 11 Knightsbridge, SW1.
▪▪ 0830-2400. U Hyde Park Corner.
This pizza restaurant has excellent jazz bands playing Mon.-Sat.

BULL'S HEAD 373 Lonsdale Rd, Barnes, SW13.
▪▪ Music 2030 Mon.-Sat., 1230 Sun. BR Barnes Bridge. ● £3-5.
This riverside pub is a jazz connoisseur's delight. Excellent bands.

ROCK GARDEN 6-7 The Piazza, Covent Garden, WC2.
▪ Music 1930-0300 Mon.-Sat., 1930-2400 Sun. U Covent Gdn. ● £5-7.
Pioneering rock venue (U2 and Dire Straits played here) with a lively bar and diner (half-price admission with meal).

MARQUEE 105 Charing Cross Rd, WC2.
▪ 1900-2300. U Leicester Sq., Tottenham Court Rd. ● £3.50-6.
Some of the world's greatest bands (The Stones, The Who, Jimi Hendrix) first made a name for themselves at the Marquee.

DINGWALLS Camden Lock, Chalk Farm, NW1.
▪ 2000-0200 Mon. & Wed., 2200-0300 Tue. & Thu.-Sat., 2000-2300 Sun. U Camden Town. ● £2-6.
Major rock and pop venue. Free on Sat. (rock), Sun. lunchtimes (jazz).

TOWN & COUNTRY CLUB 9-17 Highgate Rd, NW5.
▪ Music 2100-2300 Mon.-Thu. & Sat., 2100-0200 Fri. U Kentish Town.
● £6-10.
The best rock venue in London: ideal size, good sound, major acts.

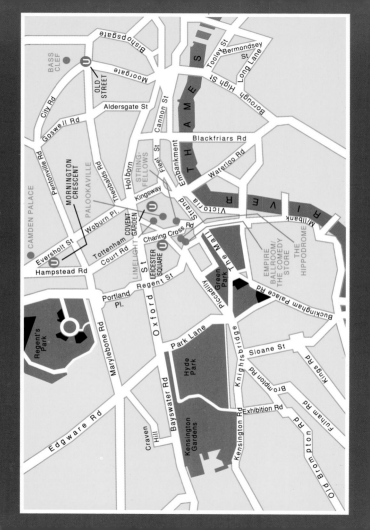

NIGHTLIFE

STRINGFELLOWS 16-19 St. Martin's Lane, WC2.
■ 2330-0330 Mon.-Sat. U Leicester Sq. ● £8-15.
Fashionable venue often frequented by the rich and famous.

THE HIPPODROME Charing Cross Rd and Cranbourne St, WC2.
■ 2100-0300 Mon.-Sat. U Leicester Sq. ● £6-12.
Popular venue with massive sound system, lasers, etc. Commercial-orientated dance for locals and smart-dressed tourists.

CAMDEN PALACE Camden High St, NW1.
■ 2100-0230 Mon.-Sat. U Mornington Crescent, Camden Town.
● £4-10.
One of London's most popular clubs with tourists. Commercial dance.

EMPIRE BALLROOM Leicester Sq., WC2.
■ 0830-0200 Mon.-Wed., 0830-0300 Thu.-Sat. U Leicester Sq. ● £5-8.
One of Europe's largest discos, featuring spectacular lighting, a revolving stage and plush surroundings.

THE COMEDY STORE Leicester Sq., WC2.
■ Performances 2000 Tue.-Thu. & Sun.; 2000 & 2400 Fri. & Sat.
U Leicester Sq. ● £6-7.
The mecca of alternative comedy in Britain. Brilliant improvisation.

PALOOKAVILLE 13a St. James's St, WC1.
■ 1730-0130 Mon.-Sat., 1900-0030 Sun. U Covent Garden. ● Free.
Restaurant/wine bar decorated in New York club style, with live jazz.

LIMELIGHT 136 Shaftesbury Ave, WC2.
■ 2200-0300 Mon.-Sat., 1900-0200 Sun. U Leicester Sq. ● £7-10.
Stylish interior converted from church. Very lively at weekends.

BASS CLEF 35 Coronet St, N1.
■ 0730-0200 Mon.-Sat., 1200-1500 (free), 1930-2400 Sun. U Old St.
● £3.50-6.50.
Atmospheric small club dedicated to jazz, funk, latin and world sounds.

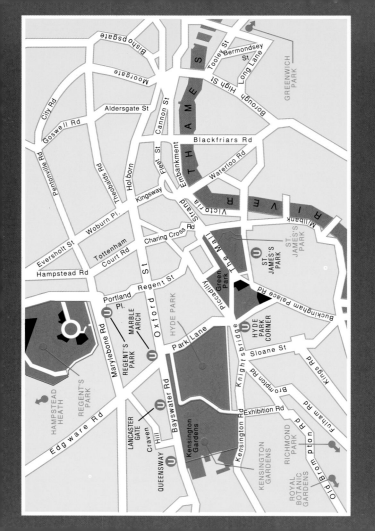

PARKS

HYDE PARK W2.
U Hyde Park Corner, Marble Arch, Queensway, Lancaster Gate.
Largest of the central parks, offering many activities. See WALK 1, **A-Z**.

KENSINGTON GARDENS SW2.
U Lancaster Gate, Queensway.
Visit the Round Pond, the statue of Peter Pan and Kensington Palace (see **A-Z**).

ST. JAMES'S PARK SW2.
U St. James's Park.
The oldest and prettiest of the central parks, with beautiful gardens and wonderful views from the bridge in the lake. See WALK 1.

REGENT'S PARK NW1.
U Regent's Park, Camden Town.
Enjoy a quiet stroll or hear Shakespeare on summer evenings. See **A-Z**.

GREENWICH PARK SE10.
BR Greenwich, Maze Hill.
This park's splendid situation high above the river affords a panoramic city view. See WALK 4, **Greenwich**.

RICHMOND PARK Richmond, Surrey.
BR/U Richmond, then Bus 65 or 71.
Largest of the royal parks, where herds of red and fallow deer roam freely amid the scenic woodland.

HAMPSTEAD HEATH NW3.
U Hampstead, Belsize Park. BR Gospel Oak, Hampstead Heath.
Wild, open heath and woodland with impressive views of London and beyond. One of London's favourite places for a day out. See **A-Z**.

ROYAL BOTANIC GARDENS Kew, Surrey.
■ See EXCURSIONS 1 for opening times, admission fees & access details.
One of the greatest plant collections in Europe. See EXCURSIONS 1.

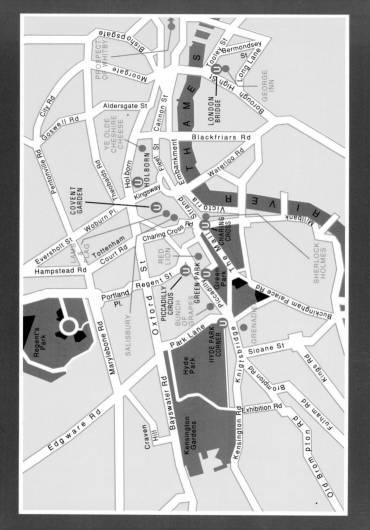

YE OLDE CHESHIRE CHEESE Wine Office Court, off Fleet St, EC4. ■ See **Opening Times**. U Temple (Sun. Holborn).
Marvellous atmospheric inn patronized by Dickens and Dr Johnson.

PROSPECT OF WHITBY 57 Wapping Wall, E1.
■ See **Opening Times**. U Wapping.
Famous East End riverside pub built in 1520, with a history of pirates and smugglers. Often overcrowded but worthwhile.

SHERLOCK HOLMES 10 Northumberland St, WC2.
■ See **Opening Times**. U Charing Cross.
Includes an interesting small 'museum' devoted to the great detective.

LAMB & FLAG Rose St, WC2.
■ See **Opening Times**. U Covent Garden.
Oldest and most atmospheric pub in Covent Garden; always crowded.

RED LION 2 Duke of York St, SW1.
■ See **Opening Times**; closed Sun. U Piccadilly Circus.
Superb miniature Victorian 'gin palace', all mahogany and cut glass.

GRENADIER 18 Wilton Row, SW1.
■ See **Opening Times**. U Hyde Park Corner.
Charming haunted pub located in a mews. Excellent bar food.

SALISBURY Cecil Court, St. Martin's Lane, W1.
■ See **Opening Times**. U Charing Cross, Leicester Sq.
Beautiful Art Nouveau décor and a cosmopolitan atmosphere.

GEORGE INN 77 Borough High St, SE1.
■ See **Opening Times**. U London Bridge.
London's last surviving galleried coaching inn, dating from 1676.

BUNCH OF GRAPES 16 Shepherd Market, W1.
■ See **Opening Times**. U Green Park.
*Traditional Victorian pub in the heart of Mayfair (see **A-Z**).*

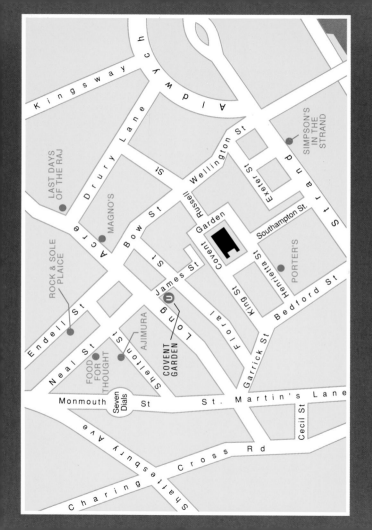

RESTAURANTS 1

MAGNO'S 65a Long Acre, WC2, tel: 071-8366077.
■ 1200-1430, 1800-2330 Mon.-Fri., 1800-2330 Sat. U Covent Garden.
● Expensive.
Traditional-style French brasserie with excellent pre-theatre menu.

SIMPSON'S IN THE STRAND 100 The Strand, WC2,
tel: 071-8369112. ■ 1200-1500, 1800-2200 Mon.-Sat. U Charing
Cross. ● Expensive. Jacket and tie for men.
The real taste of Old England – roast beef, Aylesbury duck and spotted dick. See **WALK 2**.

AJIMURA 51-53 Shelton St, WC2, tel: 071-2409424.
■ 1200-1500, 1800-2300 Mon.-Fri., 1800-2300 Sat., 1800-2230 Sun.
U Covent Garden. ● Moderate-expensive.
Japanese cuisine. Specialities for the initiated and good-value set meals.

LAST DAYS OF THE RAJ 22 Drury Lane, WC2,
tel: 071-8365705. ■ 1200-1430, 1730-2330 Mon.-Sat., 1800-2330
Sun. U Covent Garden, Holborn. ● Moderate.
Well-established, successful Indian cooperative serving a high standard of sophisticated Bengali dishes.

PORTER'S 17 Henrietta St, WC2, tel: 071-8366466.
■ 1200-2330 Mon.-Sat., 1200-2230 Sun. U Covent Garden.
● Moderate.
The traditional English pie restaurant revived, Porter's menu lists just seven pies plus desserts. Lively, mixed crowd.

ROCK & SOLE PLAICE 47 Endell St, WC2.
■ 1130-2230 (2315 takeaway) Mon.-Sat. U Covent Gdn. ● Inexpensive.
This is the spot to find good old-fashioned crunchy-battered fish and chunky chips. Eat in or take away.

FOOD FOR THOUGHT 31 Neal St, WC2, tel: 071-8360239.
■ 1200-2000 Mon.-Sat. U Covent Garden. ● Inexpensive. Unlicensed.
Popular vegetarian restaurant. Delicious salads, soups and pasta dishes.

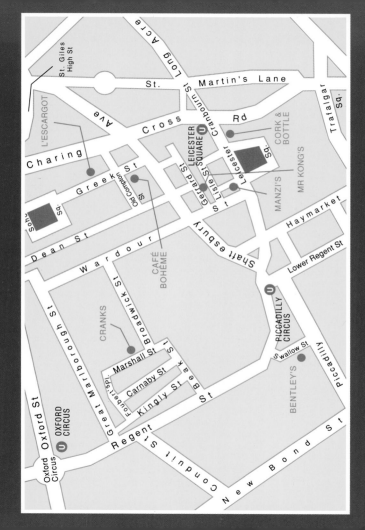

L'ESCARGOT 48 Greek St, W1, tel: 071-4372679.
■ 1200-1500, 1730-2315 Mon.-Fri., 1800-2315 Sat. U Tottenham
Court Rd, Leicester Sq. ● Expensive.
*Refined modern French cuisine which has been adapted to London
tastes. Choose from the menu in the brasserie or the main restaurant.*

BENTLEY'S 11 Swallow St, W1, tel: 071-7344756.
■ 1200-1500, 1800-2300 Mon.-Sat. U Piccadilly Circus. ● Expensive.
Jacket and tie for men.
One of the best seafood restaurant and oyster bars in town.

MANZI'S 1 Leicester St, WC2, tel: 071-7340224.
■ 1200-1430, 1730-2315 Mon.-Sat., 1800-2200 Sun. U Leicester Sq.
● Moderate.
Long-established family-run Italian seafood restaurant.

MR KONG'S 21 Lisle St, WC2, tel: 071-4377341.
■ 1200-0200. U Leicester Sq. ● Moderate.
*A pioneer of Cantonese cooking in London, offering excellent house
specialities.*

CORK & BOTTLE 44-46 Cranbourn St, WC2, tel: 071-7347807.
■ 1100-2300 Mon.-Sat., 1900-2230 Sun. U Leicester Sq. ● Inexpensive.
*Wine bar offering a variety of delicious buffet meals and an impressive
wine list.*

CAFÉ BOHÊME 13 Old Compton St, W1, tel: 071-4371503.
■ 0800-0100 Mon.-Sat., 1100-2200 Sun. U Tottenham Court Road,
Leicester Sq. ● Inexpensive.
French-style brasserie but serving some pasta dishes too.

CRANKS 8 Marshall St, W1, tel: 071-4379431, and branches.
■ 0800-2230 Mon.-Fri., 0900-2230 Sat. U Oxford Circus.
● Inexpensive.
*London's most famous vegetarian restaurants. Their soups and cakes are
particularly good.*

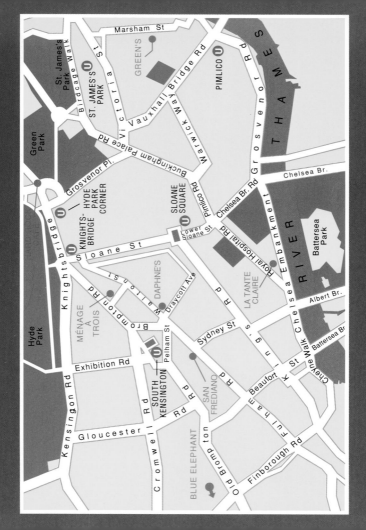

LA TANTE CLAIRE 68 Royal Hospital Rd, SW3, tel: 071-3526045.
■ 1230-1400, 1900-2300 Mon.-Fri. U Sloane Sq. ● Very Expensive.
Jacket and tie for men.
Renowned modern French cuisine. Two Michelin stars.

GREEN'S Marsham Court, Marsham St, SW1, tel: 071-8349552.
■ 1215-1430, 1830-2300 Mon.-Fri., 1830-2300 Sat. U Westminster,
Pimlico. ● Very Expensive.
Superb traditional English dishes in the style of Lockett's, the previous
hosts here. Still popular with MPs from the nearby House of Commons.

BLUE ELEPHANT 4-6 Fulham Broadway, SW6, tel: 071-3856595.
■ 1200-1430, 1900-2330 Sun.-Fri., 1900-2330 Sat. U Fulham
Broadway. ● Very Expensive.
Thai food for the European palate. Wonderfully ornate décor.

DAPHNE'S 112 Draycott Ave, SW3, tel: 071-5894257.
■ 1230-1430, 1930-2330 Mon.-Sat., 1230-1500 Sun. U South
Kensington. ● Expensive.
Classical and inventive French dishes. Smart but unpretentious.

MÉNAGE À TROIS 15 Beauchamp Pl., SW3, tel: 071-5894252.
■ 1130-1445, 1900-0015 Mon.-Fri., 1900-0015 Sat., 1900-2300 Sun.
U Knightsbridge. ● Expensive.
The international cuisine at this celebrated basement restaurant is light,
fresh and luxurious. Portions are intentionally small.

SAN FREDIANO 62 Fulham Rd, SW3, tel: 071-5848375.
■ 1230-1430, 1915-2315 Mon.-Sat., 1230-1430 Sun. U South
Kensington. ● Moderate.
Exquisite and inventive Tuscan cuisine. Excellent service.

HARD ROCK CAFÉ 150 Old Park Lane, W1.
■ 1200-0030 Mon.-Thu. & Sun., 1200-0100 Sat. U Hyde Park Corner.
● Inexpensive. No bookings. Disabled.
Legendary queues, rock memorabilia, burgers and steaks!

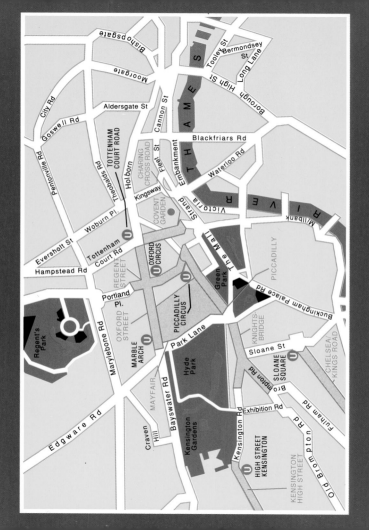

Areas

OXFORD STREET U Oxford Circus, Bond St, Marble Arch.
Britain's busiest shopping street features Selfridges (see SHOPPING 2) and several other major department stores.

COVENT GARDEN U Covent Garden.
Dominated by the shopping piazza in the former fruit-and-vegetable market. Quality boutiques and speciality shops predominate. See A-Z.

KNIGHTSBRIDGE U Knightsbridge.
Knightsbridge is synonymous with Harrods (see SHOPPING 2) which sets the standard for shops here. Good boutiques around Beauchamp Pl.

KENSINGTON HIGH STREET U High St Kensington.
Similar range of chain and clothes stores to the West End. Don't miss the designer fashions at Hyper-Hyper.

CHELSEA/KINGS ROAD U Sloane Sq.
Not the definitive fashion area it once was but still well worth an outing on a Sat. afternoon. See A-Z.

PICCADILLY U Piccadilly, Green Park.
The elegantly time-warped Jermyn St and St. James's St make Piccadilly synonymous with high-class gentlemen's shopping. See A-Z.

CHARING CROSS ROAD U Tottenham Court Rd, Leicester Sq.
Book shops galore, from Foyle's, the world's largest, to the delightful second-hand and specialist antiquarians in Cecil Court.

REGENT STREET U Piccadilly Circus, Oxford Circus.
The up-market ambience of this grand street is typified in the gleam of Garrards, the crown jewellers, and the style and elegance of Liberty (see SHOPPING 2).

MAYFAIR U Bond St.
Old and New Bond Sts, Savile Row and Burlington Arcade emphasize traditional British goods. Several small art galleries here too. See A-Z.

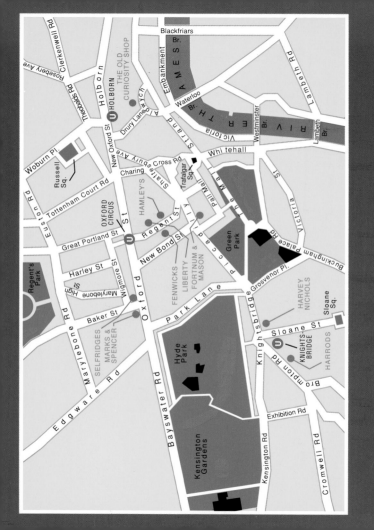

Shops

HARRODS 87 Brompton Rd, SW1.
◼ 0900-1800 Mon.-Tue., Thu.-Sat., 0930-1900 Wed. Ⓤ Knightsbr. Dis.
You can buy almost anything from Harrods. Don't miss the food halls.

HARVEY NICHOLS Knightsbridge, W1.
◼ 1000-1900 Mon.-Fri., 1000-1800 Sat. Ⓤ Knightsbridge.
High-quality store renowned for its household furnishings and fashions.

LIBERTY 210-20 Regent St, W1.
◼ 0930-1800 Mon.-Wed., Fri., Sat., 0930-1930 Thu. Ⓤ Oxford Circus.
Galleried store specializing in textiles, jewellery, china and oriental rugs.

MARKS & SPENCER 173 & 458 Oxford St, W1.
◼ 0900-2000 Mon.-Fri., 0900-1800 Sat. Ⓤ Oxford Circus, Bond St.
Famous for good-quality fashionable clothing at very reasonable prices.

SELFRIDGES 400 Oxford St, W1.
◼ 0930-1800 Mon.-Wed., Fri. & Sat., 0930-2000 Thu. Ⓤ Marble Arch.
Second-largest of London's department stores. Good food section.

FORTNUM & MASON 181 Piccadilly, W1.
◼ 0900-1730 Mon.-Sat. Ⓤ Piccadilly Circus.
The aristocrat of grocers. Exotic preserves and other epicurean delicacies.

HAMLEY'S 188 Regent St, W1.
◼ 0930-1800 Mon.-Sat., 0930-2000 Thu. Ⓤ Oxford Circus. Disabled.
World's largest toy shop, with five floors of fun for children of all ages.

FENWICKS 63 New Bond St, W1.
◼ 0930-1800 Mon.-Wed., Fri. & Sat., 0930-1930 Thu. Ⓤ Bond St.
Quality goods ranging from clothing to cookware.

THE OLD CURIOSITY SHOP 13-14 Portsmouth St, WC2.
◼ 0930-1730 Mon.-Fri., 0930-1600 Sat. & Sun. (April-Oct.); 0930-1700 Mon.-Fri., 0930-1600 Sat. & Sun. (Nov.-Mar.). Ⓤ Holborn.
The quaintest and oldest shop in town, built in 1567. Pure Dickens.

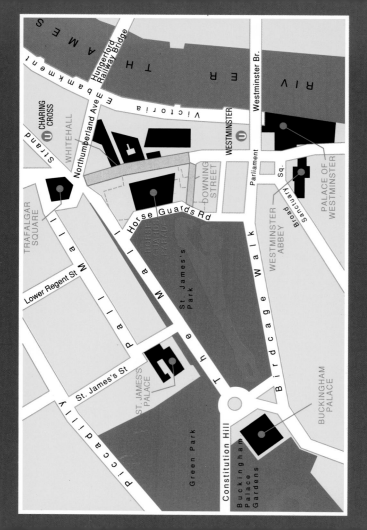

BUCKINGHAM PALACE The Mall, SW1.
■ Closed to the public except for the Queen's Gallery (see **ART GALLERIES**) and Royal Mews. U Victoria, Hyde Park Corner.
*Official residence of the monarch since Queen Victoria (see **A-Z**). When the royal standard is flying, the queen is in residence. See **WALK 1**, **A-Z**.*

PALACE OF WESTMINSTER Parliament Sq., SW1.
U Westminster.
*Home of the 'mother of parliaments'. Access to the buildings is restricted for security reasons. See **WALK 1**, **A-Z**.*

TRAFALGAR SQUARE SW1.
U Charing Cross.
*London's most famous square, with the 167 ft-high Nelson's Column, fountains, the National Gallery (see **ART GALLERIES**, **A-Z**) and the Queen's parish church, St. Martin-in-the-Fields (see **CULTURE**). See **WALK 1**, **A-Z**.*

ST. JAMES'S PALACE Pall Mall, SW1.
■ Closed to the public. U Green Park.
Formerly the favourite royal palace, St. James's now houses royal offices and Clarence House, the home of HM The Queen Mother.

WHITEHALL & HORSE GUARDS PARADE
U Charing Cross, Westminster.
*Ministry offices at the centre of British government. See the Household Cavalry on sentry duty in Whitehall (see **A-Z**). See **WALK 1**.*

WESTMINSTER ABBEY Broad Sanctuary, SW1.
■ For opening times & admission fees, see **CHURCHES**. U Westminster.
*See Poets' Corner, the Tomb of the Unknown Warrior, the Coronation Throne and the Royal Chapels. See **WALK 1**, **A-Z**.*

DOWNING STREET SW1.
■ Closed to the public. U Westminster, Charing Cross.
*No. 10 has been the official residence of the prime minister since 1735. The chancellor of the exchequer's residence is No. 11. See **WALK 1**.*

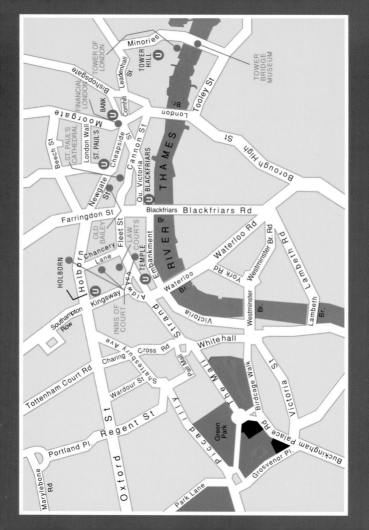

TOWER OF LONDON Tower Hill, EC1.
■ 0930-1800 Mon.-Sat., 1400-1800 Sun. (Mar.-Oct.); 0930-1700
Mon.-Sat. (Nov.-Feb.). U Tower Hill. ● £6.40, OAP £4.80, child 5-15
£3.90, family (2+3) £17.50.
*Formerly a fortress, a palace and a prison, the tower now houses the
Crown Jewels and the valuable Royal Armouries. See* **WALK 3**, **A-Z**.

TOWER BRIDGE MUSEUM
■ Museum 1000-1830 April-Oct., 1000-1645 Nov.-Mar. U Tower Hill.
● £2.50, OAP/child 5-15 £1. Disabled.
*Built in 1894, this is one of the most photographed sights in London. The
overhead walkways give splendid views along the Thames. See* **A-Z**.

LAW COURTS (Royal Courts of Justice) The Strand, WC2.
■ 0930-1630 Mon.-Fri. (Oct.-July). U Temple.
England's main civil-law courts. Trials open to the public (aged 14+).

OLD BAILEY (Central Criminal Court) Old Bailey/Newgate St, EC4.
■ 1030-1300, 1400-1600 Mon.-Fri. (mid Sep.-July). U St. Paul's.
Highest criminal court in England. Trials open to the public (aged 14+).

ST. PAUL'S CATHEDRAL Ludgate Hill, EC4.
■ 0730-1800. U St. Paul's.
*London's most enduring landmark. Don't miss the dome and its famous
Whispering Gallery. See* **CHURCHES**, **WALK 3**, **A-Z**.

FINANCIAL LONDON EC2.
U Bank.
*See the Bank of England Museum, the Stock Exchange floor, the Royal
Exchange floor and Mansion House. See* **WALK 3**.

INNS OF COURT Gray's Inn, WC1, Lincoln's Inn, WC2, Middle
Temple and Inner Temple, EC4. U Chancery Lane, Holborn, Temple
(Sun. Embankment).
*The historic training grounds of barristers for the English High Court.
Public access is available to the grounds and certain buildings. See* **A-Z**.

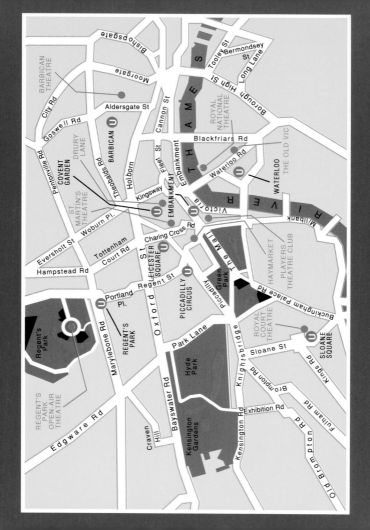

ROYAL NATIONAL THEATRE South Bank Centre, SE1,
tel: 071-9282252. BR/U Waterloo. Disabled.
The very best of international and British productions are staged in the Lyttelton, Olivier and Cottesloe theatres.

ROYAL COURT THEATRE Sloane Sq., SW1, tel: 071-7301745.
U Sloane Sq.
London's oldest avant-garde theatre; premiered works by Shaw, Osborne.

BARBICAN THEATRE Barbican Centre, EC2, tel: 071-6283351.
U Barbican (Sun. Moorgate). Disabled.
London home of the Royal Shakespeare Company. See **Barbican Centre***.*

HAYMARKET (Theatre Royal), Haymarket, SW1, tel: 071-9308800.
U Piccadilly Circus.
This elegant theatre stages classical and modern plays.

PLAYERS THEATRE CLUB The Arches, Villiers St, WC2, tel: 071-8391134. Supper bar until 0300. BR/U Charing Cross, Embankment.
Preserving the tradition of Victorian music-hall variety entertainment.

DRURY LANE (Theatre Royal), Catherine St, WC2,
tel: 071-8363687. U Covent Garden.
The oldest surviving theatre in London. Musicals are its speciality.

THE OLD VIC Waterloo Rd, SE1, tel: 071-9287616.
U Waterloo.
Lovely early-19thC theatre producing British and European classics.

ST. MARTIN'S THEATRE West St, Cambridge Circus,
tel: 071-8361443. U Leicester Sq.
For Agatha Christie-lovers – The Mousetrap has played here since 1952.

REGENT'S PARK OPEN-AIR THEATRE Inner Circle, Regent's Park, NW1, tel: 071-4862431. U Regent's Park.
The summer Shakespeare season is not to be missed.

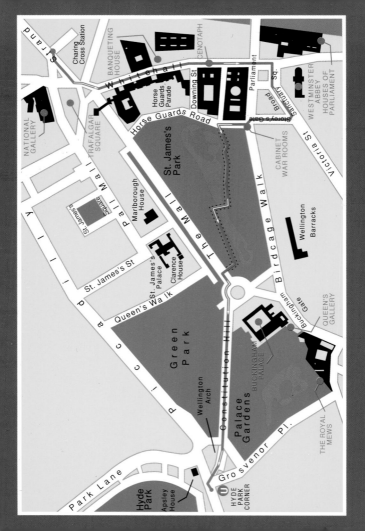

Westminster

For details of many of the attractions on the walk, see SIGHTSEEING 1.
Best days for this walk are Wed. and Thu. for the Royal Mews.

Begin at Charing Cross station. On the forecourt is a replica of the
original Charing Cross (1290) which marked the last stop of the funeral
cortege of Eleanor, wife of Edward I. Turn left down The Strand, then
left again to the top of Whitehall (see **A-Z**). From here, look across the
statues, fountains, stone lions and pigeons of Trafalgar Sq. (see **A-Z**) to
the National Gallery (see **ART GALLERIES**, **A-Z**). Go down Whitehall to
the Banqueting House (1000-1700 Mon.-Sat., 1400-1700 Sun.; £2,
OAP £1.50, child 5-15 £1.35), designed by Inigo Jones in 1622 as part
of the Palace of Whitehall. The magnificent Rubens ceiling was
commissioned by Charles I in 1629 and it was outside Banqueting
House that he was executed in 1649. Cross Whitehall to the entrance
of Horse Guards Parade, where you can see mounted sentries of the
Household Cavalry (1100-1600 Mon.-Sat., 1000-1600 Sun.). Continue
down Whitehall past the Cabinet Office, a huge 19thC structure where
the government's cabinet (inner committee) sits. Opposite is the
Ministry of Defence. Next on the right is Downing St (see **SIGHTSEEING
1**); No. 10, the London residence of the prime minister, is identifiable
by the single protruding lamp over its porch, and it is generally guarded
by a policeman. Whitehall ends at the Cenotaph which commemorates
the dead of both world wars. Parliament St begins here and at its end
stands the Palace of Westminster (see **A-Z**), better known as the Houses
of Parliament, and the clock tower known as Big Ben (see **A-Z**). Walk
round Parliament Sq. and turn left into Broad Sanctuary; ahead is
Westminster Abbey (see **CHURCHES**, **A-Z**). Cross over to Storey's Gate
and on to Horse Guards Rd. At the entrance to King Charles St are the
Cabinet War Rooms, Churchill's underground command centre (1000-
1800; £3.60, OAP £2.70, child 5-16 £1.80. Disabled). Cross into St.
James's Park (see **PARKS**) and walk round the lake. Go over the bridge,
into The Mall, and on to Buckingham Palace (see **SIGHTSEEING 1**, **A-Z**).
Visit the Queen's Gallery (see **ART GALLERIES**) or see the carriage
collection in the Royal Mews (1400-1600 Wed. & Thu.; £2, OAP
£1.50, child 5-16 £1) before walking up Constitution Hill and across
Hyde Park Corner to reach the park (see **PARKS**, **A-Z**).

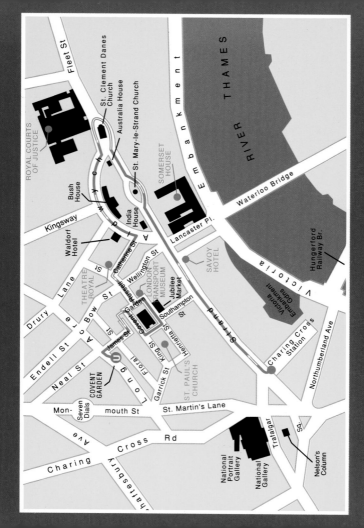

Covent Garden

Best day for this walk is Sun.

Begin at Charing Cross station. Turn right out of the forecourt and walk up The Strand past the Adelphi and Vaudeville theatres. Further along on the right, down a short lane, is the entrance to the Savoy Hotel and Theatre. The present hotel was constructed in 1889 on the site of the Earl of Savoy's 13thC palace. Further along is Simpson's in the Strand (see **RESTAURANTS 1**).

Cross over the approach road to Waterloo Bridge to reach Somerset House. Constructed on the site of a former Tudor palace, this 18thC building contains government offices and the art collection of the Courtauld Institute (see **ART GALLERIES**, **A-Z**). Carry on past King's College and the Baroque church of St. Mary-le-Strand, then cut diagonally across The Strand past St. Clement Danes, the church of the RAF, and on to the Royal Courts of Justice (popularly known as the Law Courts – see **SIGHTSEEING 2** – the civil equivalent of the Old Bailey) with their ornate Gothic façade. At the east end of the Law Courts is the Temple Bar monument which marks the boundary between Westminster and the City of London (see **A-Z**). To cross this point, traditionally, the reigning monarch has to be met by the Lord Mayor of London and given his or her permission to enter the City!

Turn back and go onto the crescent of Aldwych. On the opposite side are Australia House, Bush House (home of the BBC World Service) and India House. Cross over Kingsway, then continue past the Waldorf Hotel before turning right into Catherine St and on up to the Theatre Royal, Drury Lane (see **THEATRES**). Turn left into Russell St. Ahead is Covent Garden (see **A-Z**), which was a thriving wholesale market for fruit, vegetables and flowers as recently as 1974. Go past the London Transport Museum (see **MUSEUMS 2**) and the Jubilee Market (see **MARKETS**), and on the far side of the square is St. Paul's Church (the 'Actors' church'), designed by Inigo Jones in 1633. The first Punch-and-Judy show seen in Britain was performed in front of it in 1662 and today it is still a focus for street entertainment (see **Events**). Go inside the church (side entrance off King St) to see the memorials and graves of famous actors. Continue up James St to finish at Covent Garden underground station.

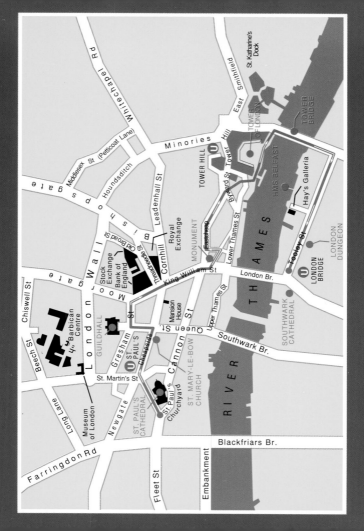

The City

Best days for this walk are Mon.-Fri. See **City**.

Begin at St. Paul's Cathedral (see **CHURCHES**, **SIGHTSEEING 2**, **A-Z**) and walk across Paternoster Sq. to St. Paul's underground station. Follow Cheapside towards the steeple of St. Mary-le-Bow, another Wren (see **A-Z**) masterpiece (1683). Cross over Cheapside and turn left into Kingly St to Gresham St. The church of St. Lawrence Jewry was built on the site of the Jewish quarter in the 17thC. Adjacent is the Guildhall, seat of the City of London's local government. The Great Hall is open to visitors (1000-1700; free) except when council meetings are in progress. There is also a clock museum in the library (entrance on Aldermanbury round the corner: 0930-1700 Mon.-Fri.; free). Turn left down Gresham St then follow Princes St to the Bank of England. You can visit its museum whose entrance is in Bartholomew Lane (1000-1700 Mon.-Fri., 1100-1700 Sun & BH; free). Opposite the Bank is the Royal Exchange, built 1842-44, where you may be able to see trading on the floor (1100-1400 Mon.-Fri.; see **SIGHTSEEING 2**). Across from the Royal Exchange is Mansion House, the official residence of the Lord Mayor of London (closed to the public). Go under the subway and up into King William St, past the church of St. Mary Woolnoth (1716-24) and under the next subway to Monument underground station. Turning first left into Monument St leads you to the Monument (see **A-Z**) commemorating the Great Fire of London in 1666. Turn left into Pudding Lane, site of the baker's shop where the great fire started. Turn right into Eastcheap and carry on to the next subway which leads straight on to the Tower of London (see **SIGHTSEEING 2**, **A-Z**). Cross Tower Bridge (see **A-Z**) then turn right into Tooley St. Walk along Tooley St and into Battlebridge Lane which leads to Hay's Galleria, a converted dock and warehouse with some interesting shops. This also leads to HMS *Belfast* (see **MUSEUMS 2**). On the opposite side of Tooley St is the London Dungeon (see **MUSEUMS 1**). Cut across London Bridge (see **A-Z**) to Southwark Cathedral (see **CHURCHES**), turn left down Borough High St to the George Inn (see **PUBS**) and finish the walk at London Bridge underground station.

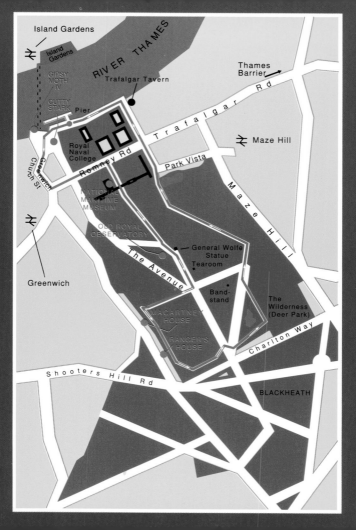

WALK 4

Greenwich Park

5 miles from central London. To get there, see **Greenwich***. Best days for this walk are Mon.-Wed. and Fri.*

Begin at Greenwich Pier and board the *Cutty Sark,* a beautiful example of a 19thC tea clipper (1000-1800 Mon.-Sat., 1200-1800 Sun., April-Sep.; 1000-1700 Mon.-Sat., 1200-1700 Sun., Oct.-Mar.; £2.50, OAP/child 7-16 £1.25). You can also visit *Gipsy Moth IV,* the vessel which Sir Francis Chichester sailed single-handed round the world in 1966-67 (same hours as *Cutty Sark*; 50p, child 5-16 30p). To the left is the entrance to the Royal Naval College with its magnificent Painted Hall (1430-1700 Fri.-Wed.; free). Walk up Greenwich Church St past the tourist office to the excellent daily market. Turn left into Nelson Rd/Romney Rd to the National Maritime Museum (1000-1800 Mon.-Sat., 1400-1800 Sun., April-Sep.; 1000-1700 Mon.-Sat., 1400-1700 Sun., Oct.-Mar.; £3.95*, OAP/child 7-16 £2.50). Before walking up the hill to the Old Royal Observatory, visit the wonderfully restored Queen's House. The observatory (opening times and admission charges* for both as Maritime Museum) is now a museum housing a collection of remarkable astronomical instruments and here you can straddle the famous Greenwich Meridian. On the roof the time ball – a signal to Thames shipping in the past – falls at 1300 each day. Follow Blackheath Ave to the tearoom where you can stop for refreshment. Turn right and head for Macartney House (closed to the public), family home of Gen. James Wolfe who left here for Quebec in 1759. His statue stands close to the observatory. Turn left to go up to the Ranger's House. Built in 1688, it is home to the Suffolk Collection of Jacobean portraits (1000-1800 summer, 1000-1600 winter; free). Go back across the park to the area known as The Wilderness. Here are squirrels, ducks and deer, and colourful flowerbeds in summer. Head down the hill towards the gate at Park Row, down to the Trafalgar Tavern, then left for a pleasant riverside stroll by the college. The walk ends back at the pier from where boat trips depart to the Thames Barrier (see **A-Z**).

*Prices shown are per individual attraction. If you plan to visit more than one a ticket for the museum, observatory and Queen's House costs £6.95, OAP/child 7-16 £4.95, family (2+5) £13.95.

Big Ben

Antiques & Auction Houses: London is a mecca for collectors, as the availability of antiques in the capital is second to nowhere else in Britain. Bond St and Knightsbridge have large numbers of expensive antique shops while, at the other end of the scale, many market stalls sell bric-a-brac, coins, stamps and all kinds of memorabilia of interest to the serious collector as well as to the casual visitor (see **MARKETS**). In addition, there are indoor antique markets in King's Rd, Kensington High St and Grays Mews/Davies St, W1 (U Bond St). Equally interesting are the sales at London's famous auction houses in the West End: Christie's, 8 King St, tel: 071-8399060; Phillips, 101 New Bond St, tel: 071-6296602; Sotheby's, 34-35 New Bond St, tel: 071-4938080. Sales take place on most weekdays, with viewings every weekday and some weekends.

Barbican Centre: The Barbican Arts Centre is the largest of its kind in western Europe. Completed in 1982, its rather confusing internal lay-out contains a concert hall (the headquarters of the London Symphony Orchestra), two theatres (see **THEATRES**), one of the biggest art galleries in London, exhibiting mainly 20thC and contemporary work (1000-1845 Mon.-Sat., 1200-1745 Sun.; £4), three cinemas, a library, conference facilities and two restaurants. Free concerts and exhibitions are held daily in the foyer. See **CULTURE**.

Big Ben: The bell, weighing over 13 tons, which sounds from the clock tower at the north end of the Houses of Parliament (see **Palace of Westminster**). Its chime is known all over the world. The name 'Big Ben' is popularly applied to the clock tower itself. See **WALK 1**.

British Museum & Library: The British Museum is one of the richest and largest in the world. The collection was originally centred around the geological and zoological items bequeathed to the nation by Sir Hans Sloane in 1753. The magnificent building, with its austere classical façade, was designed by Sir Robert Smirke and built in 1823-47. It would be impossible to view all the exhibits in one or even two visits. Your best bet is to take an introductory guided tour (£5) which will acquaint you with the museum, then explore it for yourself afterwards. The several departments include Greek antiquities, Egyptian and Oriental artefacts (don't miss the mummies!), prehistoric, Roman and medieval Britain, printed books, manuscripts and drawings. Notable among the treasures are the controversial Elgin marbles, the Rosetta stone (which provided the key to deciphering hieroglyphics), Magna Carta, Sumerian antiquities (3500-1500 BC) from the city of Ur and objects from Roman and Anglo-Saxon Britain, including the Sutton Hoo and Mildenhall treasures. Every hour, on the hour, there is a brief conducted visit to the British Library to see the huge circular reading room and its magnificent dome. See **MUSEUMS 1**.

Buckingham Palace: Built originally in 1705 as the town residence of the Duke of Buckingham, the palace was remodelled in 1820 by John Nash for George IV but did not become the official home of the sovereign until 1837 when Queen Victoria (see **A-Z**) took up residence after her coronation. The front of the building looks out over a 40 acre private garden, while the back faces the Mall and overlooks the forecourt where the Changing of the Guard (see **A-Z**) attracts large crowds in summer. The State apartments are not open to visitors but works from the royal collections are displayed in the Queen's Gallery on the south side of the palace (see **ART GALLERIES**), while in the Royal Mews (further down Buckingham Palace Rd) you can see the queen's coaches, including the gold carriage used on State occasions. See **SIGHTSEEING 1, WALK 1**.

Changing of the Guard: The most famous ceremony in Britain. The responsibility for protecting the sovereign rotates among the regiments of the footguards, in combination with the horseguards of the Household Cavalry. At 1115-1120 the St. James's Palace part of the Old Guard marches down The Mall to meet the Old Guard of Buckingham Palace. There they await the arrival, at 1130, of the New Guard, with a band from Wellington Barracks. The actual change involves the ceremonial handing over of the keys of the palace and the changing of sentries at Buckingham Palace and St. James's Palace. Meanwhile, the band forms up to play a selection of informal music which may include snatches of West End shows and even pop tunes. At around 1205 when

all the sentries have been changed the (now complete) Old Guard marches out to return to Wellington Barracks and two minutes later the St. James's detachment of the New Guard marches up The Mall to return to St. James's Palace. The ceremony takes place every day, from 1 April to 31 July and every other day from 1 August to 31 March. Wet weather may cause cancellation. Make sure to get there early, as large crowds gather outside the palace gates for the best view.

Chelsea: This fashionable residential district on the north bank of the Thames has always been popular with writers and artists. Chelsea's Bohemian heritage is clearly reflected in the wealth of blue plaques along Cheyne Walk, commemorating the various personalities who have lived in the area. Its town houses have splendid Palladian façades, and Lindsay House, 95-100 Cheyne Walk, is a particularly fine example of the style, as is 24 Cheyne Row (off Cheyne Walk), the house where the writer Thomas Carlyle (1795-1881) lived from 1834 until his death (1100-1700 Wed.-Sun. & BH, April-Oct.; £2, child 5-17 £1). Adjacent to Cheyne Walk is the elegant Royal Hospital, designed by Christopher Wren (see **A-Z**), and its peaceful gardens where the Chelsea Flower Show is held (see **Events**). The hospital is the retirement home of the famous Chelsea pensioners. You can visit its museum, chapel and the Great Hall on your own, or one of these august gentlemen will no doubt be pleased to give you a guided tour. There is no charge but do give a tip (1000-1200, 1400-1600 Mon.-Sat., 1400-1600 Sun.). Almost adjacent to the Royal Hospital is the excellent National Army Museum which traces the history of the British Army from 1485 to date (1000-1730 Mon.-Sat., 1400-1730 Sun.; free. Disabled). The area is also home to the Chelsea Physic Garden, on Swan Walk (1400-1700 Wed. & Sun.; £2.50, OAP/child £1.30). This is the oldest research garden in London, predating Kew by some 86 years. And of course there are the fashionable shops of the Kings Rd (see **SHOPPING 1**).

City, The: The original 'square mile' of London, the area that the Romans called Londinium. The City is one of the world's most important financial centres, and thousands of commuters stream over London Bridge into the area each day to staff the offices of banks, stockbrokers, insurance companies and mercantile houses. By night and at weekends, however, the City depopulates to almost a ghost town, from its working population of 300,000 to just 6000 residents. The City of London has preserved its own traditions, character and form of local government. Each year a new Lord Mayor is elected by his or her fellow aldermen and sheriffs from the livery companies and the merchant guilds (whose origins date back to medieval times). In Nov. the City thrills to the pageantry of the Lord Mayor's Show, when the newly-elected mayor parades through the streets from the Guildhall to Mansion House, the mayoral residence (see **Events**). See **WALK 3**.

Cleopatra's Needle: Standing on the Thames Embankment near Victoria, this rose-granite obelisk is 68 ft high and weighs 180 tons. It has no direct connection with Queen Cleopatra, predating her by many centuries, but came from Heliopolis in Egypt and was one of a pair erected by Thothmes III in around 1500 BC as a tribute to Ra, the sun god. It was gifted to the UK in 1819 by Egypt, and erected on this spot in 1878.

Courtauld Institute Galleries: Samuel Courtauld founded the art history department of London University and in 1931 bequeathed to it his art collection, rich in Old Flemish and Italian masterpieces. In 1981 the Princes Gate Collection, including works by Brueghel the Elder and Rubens, was added. It is one of London's best galleries and is particularly strong on French postimpressionists. See **ART GALLERIES**, **WALK 2**.

Covent Garden: The site of Covent Garden was formerly owned by the Abbey of Westminster, and produce was cultivated here for the monks (its present name is a corruption of Convent Garden, 'convent' being the old term for a religious community). After the dissolution of the monasteries in 1536 the land was granted to the Dukes of Bedford and in 1627 the architect Inigo Jones was commissioned to design the first square in London. He was much influenced by the Italian style of marketplace and the name Piazza still applies to the central square. The market for fruit, vegetables and flowers was established in 1670 and the area developed alongside it. The market flourished, albeit in a very unruly manner until the early part of this century, and finally in 1974 it moved out to Nine Elms near Chelsea. The area was sensitively restored and it now houses one of the capital's most popular shopping (see **MARKETS**) and entertainment precincts. The latest addition to 'the Garden' is The Rubberworks, an exhibition of the venomous *Spitting Image* puppets (1100-1900; £2.90, OAP/child under 12 £1.90) which maintains the area's great theatrical tradition, although in this case from a very wry viewpoint! See **WALK 2**.

Dickens, Charles (1812-70): The author who described 19thC London in such vivid detail lived for two years at 48 Doughty St, WC1, now restored to house the fascinating Dickens House Museum (1000-1700 Mon.-Sat.; £2, OAP £1.50, child 5-16 £1, family 2+3 £4). It is the finest collection of Dickens memorabilia in the world, and the exhibits reflect particularly the novels he wrote during his stay here (the final instalment of *The Pickwick Papers*, *Oliver Twist*, *Nicholas Nickleby* and the start of *Barnaby Rudge*).

Docklands: This is the area downstream from Tower Bridge (see **A-Z**) which was once one of the greatest ports in the world. When the last ship departed in 1981 it left behind unemployment, a dwindling

St. Katherine's Dock

population and hundreds of acres of seemingly hopeless dereliction.
In July 1981 the London Docklands Development Corporation (LDDC)
was given the task of revitalizing the area; it is now being transformed
into a thriving commercial, residential and cultural district. Impressive
Victorian warehouses and Hawksmoor churches have been restored,
old pubs with real East End character have been preserved and a
Museum of Docklands is being established to illustrate the area's
historical importance.

The Docklands Light Railway (DLR) has been developed to serve the
area, running from Tower Gateway (close to the Tower of London) east
through Limehouse and Poplar. A trip on this is by far the best way to
see Docklands, travelling quietly and quickly on an elevated track with
a marvellous view of the futuristic buildings which grow here almost
daily. The area's centrepiece is the Canary Wharf Tower, the tallest
building in Europe at 800 ft.

The line ends at Island Gardens and a tunnel under the Thames provides pedestrian access to Greenwich. The LDDC has produced a
helpful free leaflet which outlines different walks, and comes complete
with detailed maps, which is available from most tourist information
offices (see **A-Z**).

Dulwich: This pleasant, well-heeled south London suburb (30 min by train from Victoria) is home to the Dulwich Picture Gallery. Designed by Sir John Soane (see **MUSEUMS 2**) and opened in 1814, it is England's oldest public art collection (College Rd; 1100-1700 Tue.-Sat., 1400-1700 Sun.; £1.50, OAP 50p, under 16s free. Free guided tours 1500 Sat. & Sun. Disabled). Among its notable Dutch paintings is Rembrandt's *Titus as a Young Man*, and there are fine examples of 17th and 18thC British portraiture, Italian works by Raphael and Veronese, 19thC French paintings and some superb sketches by Rubens. Close by, at Forest Hill, is another excellent local collection, the Horniman Museum. This small museum is devoted to ethnography, natural history and early musical instruments (1030-1800 Mon.-Sat., 1400-1800 Sun.; free. Disabled).

Food: English food and cooking, once much maligned, has enjoyed something of a revival in recent years. You will probably encounter at least some of the following:
Breakfast – the famous 'full English' version normally includes egg, bacon, sausage, tomato and perhaps mushrooms, black pudding (a pig's-blood sausage) and fried bread (although in these more health-

conscious days 'Continental Breakfast' is usually available also, comprising anything from tea and toast to coffee, croissant and jam).

Lunch – a Ploughman's is a typical light pub lunch consisting of bread, cheese (or ham or pâté), salad and pickle. If the bread is good and you get a good wedge of tasty farmhouse Cheddar or traditionally produced ham, this can be delicious. Try to see what it looks like before ordering. A pastie, Cornish in origin, is a pastry envelope containing vegetables and sometimes meat.

Afternoon Tea (see **Drinks**) – taken mid-late afternoon, this very English repast may include sandwiches and will certainly offer scones, eaten with jam and cream. Expect to pay around £2.50 for a 'cream tea' which comprises a pot of tea and two scones.

Dinner – traditional English dishes include: roast meats (either lamb, pork or beef, the latter being served on Sun. with Yorkshire pudding); hot pies (e.g. steak-and-kidney); cold pies (usually game); and game dishes such as duck, pheasant, partridge, venison and so on (although these are not so common and can be expensive).

Desserts – English desserts worth looking out for include: sherry trifle (a concoction of fruit, jelly and sponge fingers soaked in sherry and topped with custard and cream); fruit fool (a light dish of whipped cream and puréed fruit); fruit syllabub (similar to fool, with wine and lemon juice); and fruit crumble (stewed fruit with a crumbly pastry topping).

Finally, don't pass on the port and cheese. Stilton (blue-veined and strong) and Cheddar are the best-known but local English cheeses of every variety and provenance, including goat's and ewe's, are now very fashionable. And traditional fish 'n' chips, whether eaten in the shop or taken away wrapped in newspaper and eaten outside, is a delicacy that all foreign visitors should try. See **RESTAURANTS 1-3**, **Eating Out**.

Greenwich: Situated 5 miles downstream from London, Greenwich is famous the world over for the meridian which determines Greenwich Mean Time (GMT). You can stand astride the east-west line at the Old Royal Observatory in Greenwich Park and look over almost the whole city from the park. Exploring the *Cutty Sark*, the National Maritime

Museum and the Royal Naval College will take you the best part of a day so you'll have to return to see the market and the new Fan Museum on Crooms Hill (1400-1600 Tue., 1100-1630 Wed.-Sat., 1400-1630 Sun.; £2.50, OAP free Tue. only, otherwise as child 5-16 £1.50. Disabled). You can get to Greenwich by train from Charing Cross to Greenwich or Maze Hill (30 min) or Docklands Light Railway (DLR) link from Tower Gateway to Island Gardens (15 min), then a 10 min walk through the pedestrian tunnel. Alternatively, travel by pleasure boat from Westminster Pier (45 min), Charing Cross Pier (30 min) or Tower Pier (20 min), or by Riverbus catamaran (see **Boats**). See PARKS, WALK 4.

Hampstead: One of the most attractive 'villages' in London, Hampstead has been home to many writers and artists, including Keats, Constable and D. H. Lawrence. The district lies in the north of London, 30 min from the centre by underground (Northern line).
The pride of Hampstead is Kenwood House in Hampstead Lane, which houses the superb Iveagh Bequest collection of paintings (1000-1800 Easter/April-Sep., 1000-1600 Oct-Easter/April; free. Disabled). Summertime concerts are held in its beautiful gardens. You can also savour the luxurious surroundings of Fenton House in Hampstead Grove with its sumptuous Regency interior (1100-1700 Sat.-Wed., May-Oct.; £2.80, OAP/child 5-17 £1.40). Keats' House in Wentworth Pl. contains mementos from the poet's occupancy; during his two years there he wrote some of his most famous works, including *Ode to a Nightingale* (1400-1800 Mon.-Fri., 1000-1700 Sat., 1400-1700 Sun., April-Oct.; 1300-1700 Mon.-Fri., 1000-1700 Sat., 1400-1700 Sun., Nov.-Mar.; free). After a walk around Hampstead Heath (see PARKS) you can enjoy a relaxing drink at one of the area's many famous pubs: The Flask, in Flask Walk, whose name comes from the era when Hampstead had its own spa and assembly rooms; Jack Straw's Castle, which has a fine view from the top of the Heath and is named after a leader of the Peasants' Revolt of 1381; or the Spaniards Inn, one of the many local hostelries which Dick Turpin, the 17thC highwayman, is said to have frequented.

Hampton Court: See EXCURSIONS 1.

Holmes, Sherlock: Baker St, which runs north to south between Regent's Park and Portman Sq., is the place of pilgrimage for all fans of Sherlock Holmes, the super sleuth created by Sir Arthur Conan Doyle (1859-1930). No. 221b was the supposed address of Holmes and his colleague and chronicler, Dr Watson, but, disappointingly, the site is occupied by a branch of the Abbey National bank. However, a new Sherlock Holmes Museum has opened at 239 Baker St (1000-1800; £5, OAP/child £3), claiming that it is the real building mentioned in Conan Doyle's stories! You can see more artefacts associated with the great detective in a small museum above the Sherlock Holmes pub (see PUBS).

Houses of Parliament: See **Palace of Westminster**.

Hyde Park: The most famous and most popular of the royal parks. Hyde Park merges with Kensington Gardens and together they cover the 600 acres which were once the favourite hunting grounds of Henry VIII. The land was first opened to the public in the 17thC. Take a walk round the Serpentine Lake or along Rotten Row (used for horse riding). On Sun. (1100 onwards) visit Speakers' Corner (U Marble Arch), close to the site of the old Tyburn gallows. Today large crowds are attracted to a less gruesome spectacle – the soapbox orators voicing their opin-

ions on issues of the day. You will also find the Serpentine Gallery, a small modern-art collection (1100-1800 summer, 1100-1600 winter; free), the open-air swimming pool known as the Lido, children's play areas, rowing boats for hire (Mar.-Oct.) and tennis courts. In summer there are lunchtime concerts at the bandstand. See **PARKS**, **WALK 1**.

Imperial War Museum: The Imperial has undergone major redevelopment and is now widely recognized as London's most exciting specialist museum. Multisensory experiences of trench warfare and the Blitz combine with remarkable film and sound recordings to make for a memorable trip. Famous documents, personal letters and deadly weaponry recount the history of 20thC British warfare in a way that is compelling but never gung ho. See **MUSEUMS 2**.

Inns of Court: Perhaps London's best-kept secret, the Inns of Court are responsible for the training and appointment of barristers (i.e. those members of the legal profession entitled to plead in the English law courts). These oases of tranquillity within the heart of the bustling city resemble small university campuses and comprise rooms, which are either offices or residential quarters ('inn' meant 'house' in Old English), a hall, chapel, library and gardens. The buildings are superbly preserved and interspersed with manicured lawns and lovely gardens. There are four inns: Lincoln's Inn, the oldest and most beautiful; Gray's Inn, the smallest; Inner Temple and Middle Temple. The latter are discrete bodies but are adjacent within the area known as the Temple (formerly occupied by the medieval Knights Templar) and only the sign on the wall (a winged horse for Inner, the Lamb of God for Middle) indicates which area or building belongs to which inn. The grounds of all the inns are usually open to the public daily (Lincoln's Inn closed Sat. & Sun.) and some of the buildings are also open; ask at the gatehouse for details. It is best to take a walking tour (see **Guides**) to get the most from a visit to the Inns. See **CHURCHES**, **SIGHTSEEING 2**.

Johnson, Samuel (1709-84): The writer, lexicographer, wit and sage lived at Gough Sq. during the eight years he worked on his famous dictionary. You can visit his splendid Georgian town house and see the conditions in which he and his six clerks lived and worked (1100-1730 Mon.-Sat., May-Sep.; 1100-1700 Oct.-April; £1.50, OAP/child £1. U Temple, Chancery Lane). After your visit have a drink in his favourite inn, Ye Olde Cheshire Cheese in Wine Office Court (see **PUBS**).

Kensington: An exclusive residential and shopping district, Kensington offers a variety of activities and entertainments for visitors. South Kensington is world-famous for its museums – the Victoria and Albert (see **MUSEUMS 1**, **A-Z**), the Science Museum (see **MUSEUMS 1**, **A-Z**), and the Natural History Museum and Geological Museum (see **MUSEUMS 1**). Shops range from the grandeur of Harrods (see **SHOPPING 2**) in Brompton Rd to the antique dealers in Kensington Church St and the fashionable stalls of Kensington Market in Kensington High St. Parks include Kensington Gardens (see **PARKS**) and Holland Park, which contains the beautiful gardens in the grounds of Holland House. The Commonwealth Institute in front of Holland Park features colourful displays from each of the 48 member countries of the Commonwealth (1000-1730 Mon.-Sat., 1400-1700 Sun.; free. Disabled). Just off High St are two fascinating houses. The first is Leighton House, built 1864-66, which was the home and studio of the distinguished Victorian painter, Lord Leighton. The exotically-tiled Arab Hall centrepiece of the house is straight out of the *Arabian Nights* (1100-1700 Mon.-Sat.; free). The second, Linley Sambourne House, also built in the 1860s, is a perfectly preserved late Victorian/early Edwardian period piece with original decorations, *objets d'art* and sumptuous furnishings (1000-1600 Wed., 1400-1700 Sun., Mar.-Oct.; £2, child £1).

Kensington Palace: The asthmatic William III moved here in 1689 to escape the riverside damp of Whitehall and 300 years on it is still an inhabited royal palace, now being the London residence of the Prince and Princess of Wales. Their private apartments lie behind the State apartments which are open to the public (0900-1700 Mon.-Sat., 1300-1700 Sun.; £3.75, OAP £2.80, child 5-16 £2.50. U High St Kensington). These include Queen Victoria's bedroom (when she was Princess Victoria), the Court Dress Collection, the King's Gallery and the Council Chamber.

Kew (Royal Botanic Gardens): See EXCURSIONS 1, PARKS.

Leicester Sq.: The square was originally laid out in 1665 and gained early notoriety as a duelling ground. Today it is a throbbing central meeting point and entertainment mecca including, among other venues, four large cinemas, the Empire Ballroom (see **NIGHTLIFE**), the Comedy Store (see **NIGHTLIFE**) and the reduced-price theatre ticket booth where cheap tickets are sold for same-day performances (see **Theatres**). The theme of arts and entertainment is also reflected in the statues within the square, which include a marble bust of Shakespeare

(a copy of the original in Westminster Abbey), the painter and engraver Hogarth (who lived nearby) and the recently added bronze statue of actor and director Charlie Chaplin.

Lloyds of London: The world-famous underwriters occupy the most controversial piece of architecture in London. Designed by Richard Rogers (of Pompidou Centre fame) it has been described as a 'post-modern oil refinery' and, like Rogers' Parisian creation, it wears its pipes inside out, boilerhouse fashion. At night the illuminated arch of its 200 ft-high central atrium and the eery blue glow around it make it look like a giant, old-fashioned jukebox! A 'History of Lloyds' exhibition can be reached by taking the space-age elevators up to the fourth floor (1000-1430 Mon.-Fri.; free. Disabled. U Monument, Bank).

London Bridge: Until 1750 this was the only bridge over the Thames in London. The bridge of nursery rhyme fame was dismantled in 1968 and reconstructed in the USA. See **WALK 3**.

Mayfair: It is hard to imagine that this most fashionable residential area was once the scene of riotous and disorderly behaviour. The situation got so bad that the May Fair, after which the district was named, was banned by royal decree in the 18thC. Mayfair is now associated with elegant Georgian squares whose very names evoke quality – Berkeley, Grosvenor and Hanover. The hotels and casinos of Park Lane are world-famous but for a more informal evening here, try the cafés and restaurants around the atmospheric narrow streets and alleys of Shepherd Market. See **SHOPPING 1**.

Monument, The: Christopher Wren (see **A-Z**) and City Surveyor Robert Hooke designed this column to commemorate the Great Fire of 1666. Its height is 202 ft, which is the distance from its base to the site of the bakery in Pudding Lane where the fire started. The climb up the inside to the top is rewarded with fine views of the City skyline, more changed in the past 30 years than in the two centuries before (0900-1600 Mon.-Sat., Oct.-Mar.; 0900-1800 Mon.-Fri., 1400-1800 Sat. & Sun., April-Sep.; £1, child 5-15 25p. U Monument). See **WALK 3**.

Museum of London: This excellent museum details the history and social life of London. Prehistoric finds, Roman mosaics and temple remains, medieval coins and pottery, Tudor jewels, reminders of the Plague and the Great Fire (see **Monument**), and the London of Pepys, Hogarth and Dickens (see **A-Z**) are all here to be enjoyed. A favourite of most visitors is the Lord Mayor of London's gilded 18thC State coach which is used annually in the Lord Mayor's Show. See **MUSEUMS 1**.

National Gallery: From the relatively humble acquisition of 38 paintings by parliamentary purchase in 1824, the National Gallery now possesses over 2000 paintings, probably the best collection of European art in the world.

Periods covered range from the early Italian Renaissance to the French impressionists of the 19thC (later works of British and European art are housed in the Tate Gallery – see **A-Z**) and include celebrated works such as Leonardo's *Virgin and Child with St. John the Baptist and St. Anne* (cartoon), Ucello's *The Battle of San Romano*, Piero Della Francesca's *The Baptism of Christ* and *Christ Driving the Traders from the Temple* by El Greco. The collection was first housed in its present building in 1838, on the site of a former royal mews. There are regular guided tours as well as lectures and audio-visual displays. See **ART GALLERIES, WALK 1**.

Palace of Westminster

Palace of Westminster: Although it is better known as the Houses of Parliament, this immense Gothic edifice bordering the Thames is officially known as the New Palace of Westminster. The old palace, which was the residence of the sovereign from the 11th-15thC, was destroyed in a spectacular fire in 1834. Westminster Hall, which survived the fire, was the meeting place of the great councils of the medieval monarchs, and after 1547 became the seat of the Commons. Part of the cloisters, St. Stephen's Hall and the crypt also survived to become incorporated into the new Houses of Parliament, designed and built by Charles Barry and his assistant, Augustus Pugin, between 1840 and 1860. The porch under the Victoria Tower in the southwest corner is entered by the sovereign during the State Opening of Parliament (see **Events**). The clock tower at the north end houses Big Ben (see **A-Z**). The House of Lords has a grand Gothic hall with red leather benches. The House of Commons was destroyed during the Blitz in 1941 and rebuilt in quasi-Gothic style by Gilbert Scott.

The Public Gallery of each House is open when Parliament is in session, as follows: House of Commons 1430 onwards Mon.-Thu., 0930-1500 Fri. Prime Minister's question time takes place on Tue. and Thu. afternoons; House of Lords 1430 onwards Mon.-Wed., 1500 onwards Thu., 1100 onwards Fri. Other rooms of the palace house the members' offices and commissions as well as the magnificent library, designed by Pugin. These rooms are open to the public by guided tour only. Contact your local Member of Parliament (MP) or your embassy (see **A-Z**) for a special pass. See **SIGHTSEEING 1, WALK 1**.

Piccadilly: The area takes its name from the pickadil, a stiff collar fashionable in the 17thC when it was sold by a local merchant. Even today Piccadilly is still associated with expensive shops and snappy, though traditional dressing. Elegant Burlington Arcade, still patrolled by top-hatted beadles, was the first shopping precinct in England (1819) and typifies old-style Piccadilly. Sartorial elegance can still be acquired at a price from one of the many exclusive Savile Row tailors (see **SHOPPING 1**). Piccadilly Circus is a famous London landmark and busy traffic spot at the junction of Piccadilly, Regent St, Shaftesbury Ave and Coventry St. At night the area's sparkling neon signs illuminate throngs of revellers heading for an evening out in the West End (see **A-Z**). In the centre is a memorial to the Earl of Shaftesbury (1801-85), philanthropist and reformer, which is topped by the bronze statue popularly known as Eros (the Greek god of love), although the figure is supposed to represent the angel of Christian charity.

Adjacent, housed in the London Pavilion, is Rock Circus, featuring animated models of world-famous rock-music stars and static tableaux (1100-2100 Mon., Wed., Thu. & Sun., 1200-2100 Tue., 1100-2200 Fri. & Sat.; £6.25, OAP £5.25, child 5-13 £4.25). A big draw at the nearby Trocadero Centre, a three-storey mall, is the Guinness World of Records (see **CHILDREN**).

Pubs: No visit to London would be complete without sampling a pint of bitter in the smoky atmosphere of a traditional pub (short for 'public house'). Some pubs also have revues and theatrical entertainments or regular live music, while others double as restaurants.

The minimum legal age for someone to be served alcohol is 18 but some pubs will only serve those aged 21 or over. Children are admitted only if the pub has a 'family room', garden or separate restaurant. To enter the pub bar or lounge area the law states that children must be aged at least 14, accompanied by an adult and may not purchase or drink alcohol. A 16-year-old may drink certain alcoholic drinks in the restaurant only. Both of these are subject to the landlord's or landlady's discretion.

Prices of drinks vary but you should expect to pay about £1.50 for a pint of beer and £1.10 for a measure of spirits in a pub. See **PUBS**, **Drinks**, **Opening Times**.

Regent's Park: Surrounded by the splendid terraced houses of Park Cres., Park Sq., and York, Chester and Cumberland terraces, Regent's Park is still as John Nash designed it in 1820. The Inner Circle gives access to Queen Mary's Gardens, where Shakespeare's plays are performed in the open-air theatre on summer evenings (see **THEATRES**). Visitors to the park can stroll through the gardens, hire a boat on the lake or sit on one of the deck chairs provided and watch the birdlife in comfort. See **PARKS**.

St. Paul's Cathedral

St. Paul's Cathedral: This masterpiece by Christopher Wren (see **A-Z**) is the fourth church to stand on this site. It was the first domed church to be built in England (1675) and also the first to be built under the supervision of a single architect. Its many-splendoured features include the choir, with intricately carved stalls sculpted by Grinling Gibbons (1690), and a magnificent organ. On the south aisle of the choir stands the monument to the Metaphysical poet John Donne, Dean of St. Paul's 1620-31; this is the only statue belonging to the old cathedral to have survived the Great Fire of 1666 completely intact. Other monuments are dedicated to the Duke of Wellington, Lord Leighton, Samuel Johnson (see **A-Z**) and Joshua Reynolds. At the corner of the choir and the south transept is the entrance to the crypt, which contains the tombs of famous figures including Wellington, Nelson, Reynolds and Turner (among others, in Painters' Corner), and Wren himself. The crypt also contains the London Diocese Treasury (1000-1615 Mon.-Fri., 1100-1615 Sat.). From the south transept stairs lead up to the Whispering Gallery (opening times as for the crypt). Here there are breathtaking views of the dome murals and the choir. Visitors can also experience an amazing acoustic phenomenon which allows the slightest whisper to be heard at the opposite end of the gallery. Further up (542 steps!) is the Golden Gallery, offering thrilling panoramas over the city and the Thames. See **CHURCHES, SIGHTSEEING 2, WALK 3**.

Science Museum: This vast collection of science, industry, technology and medicine, founded in 1857, spans antiquity to the nuclear age and comprises over 100 subject collections displayed in 60 galleries on six floors. It is impossible to see everything in one visit so consider returning at least once. On the ground floor are exhibits illustrating the history and development of motive power, with early industrial engines and steam locomotives, including Stevenson's *Rocket* (1829) and the superb *Caerphilly Castle* (1923), beautifully evocative of the steam age. There are also displays on the history of road and rail transport, and space exploration. The Children's Gallery is a great favourite and allows youngsters to examine and experiment with various scientific displays and models. On the second floor there is a fine collection of model ships and displays covering chemistry, computing and nuclear physics.

Exhibits relating to medical history, inventions, photography and the film industry occupy the third floor alongside the National Aeronautical Gallery, where famous pioneering aircraft are suspended from the ceiling. On the fourth and fifth floors is the fascinating Wellcome Museum of the History of Medicine; don't miss it. See **CHILDREN**, **MUSEUMS 1**.

Soho: This district stretches from Regent St to Charing Cross Rd and from Oxford St to Shaftesbury Ave. It has long been known as central London's most cosmopolitan area and has always enjoyed a dubious reputation. However, in recent years the sex shops, saunas and peep shows have largely been replaced by bistros, restaurants and boutiques. Visit the 17thC Soho Sq., off Oxford St, near Tottenham Court Rd underground station. South of the square is Greek St, which contains one of the more interesting buildings in the area, the House of St. Barnabas (1430-1615 Wed., 1100-1230 Thu.; free), a charitable institution founded in 1846. Across Shaftesbury Ave lies the small Chinatown district, which revolves around Gerrard St and is brimming with restaurants and oriental shops. See also the lovely St. Anne's churchyard in Wardour St, overlooked by a beautiful tower, all that remained after the church was bombed in World War II. Most typical of Soho's streets are Dean St, Old Compton St, Poland St, Berwick St and Brewer St, which are filled with delicatessens, pubs and traditional grocers and butchers. At the Oxford Circus end is Carnaby St, fashion mecca of the '60s.

Chinatown, Soho

Tate Gallery: The Tate Gallery concentrates on 20thC British and international paintings and sculpture. The collection originated from the bequest of Sir Henry Tate, the sugar tycoon, in 1892. In addition to modern works the British Collection dates back to the 16thC and includes rural scenes by Constable, sporting works by Stubbs, landscapes by Gainsborough and apocalyptic works by Blake. Some of Turner's greatest works have been housed in the new Clore Gallery extension. The Modern Collection encompasses the main 20thC schools and movements. The Tate also organizes internationally-recognized exhibitions of contemporary works. The museum's restaurant has an excellent reputation and contains an interesting display of Rex Whistler murals. See **ART GALLERIES**.

Thames Barrier: Opened in 1984 by the Queen, this remarkable feat of engineering has been dubbed 'the eighth wonder of the world'. Its purpose is to protect London in the event of a flood tide. It consists of ten steel gates, each over 65 ft high, which in the lowered position lie flat against the river bed (i.e. most of the time they are submerged and invisible). When a flood tide threatens they pivot up through 90° to a vertical position. An exhibition and film show at the visitor centre explain how the barrier works (1030-1700 Mon.-Fri., 1030-1730 Sat. & Sun.; £2.25, OAP/child 5-16 £1.40). It can be reached by train from Charing Cross or by boat from one of the central London piers or Greenwich Pier (see **Boats**). See WALK 4.

Tower Bridge: One of the most photographed sights in London, this massive drawbridge was built 1886-94 and designed by Sir Horace Jones and Sir John Wolfe Barry. Its innards now house the excellent Tower Bridge Museum (see SIGHTSEEING 2). The walkways which span the top of the bridge were designed to allow pedestrians to cross when the drawbridges were raised. They provide magnificent views up and down the river. The exhibition areas inside the tower describe the history of the bridge, working models demonstrate its operation and below

in the engine rooms is the original hydraulic machinery which powered the bridge prior to the installation of electrical equipment in 1976. See **WALK 3**.

Tower of London: This 900-year-old legend has served as a garrison, menagerie, royal residence and prison since it was built by William the Conqueror in 1097. Today it is one of the city's most popular tourist attractions despite, or perhaps because of, its dismal and bloody history.

The tower is guarded by the Yeomen Warders (known as Beefeaters) in their distinctive Tudor uniforms. Join one of their number for a free and highly entertaining tour (departing continuously). On Tower Green is a plaque bearing the names of some of the famous royal victims of the executioner's blade, including Anne Boleyn (1536) and Lady Jane Grey (1554), and Elizabeth I's former favourite, Robert Devereux, Earl of Essex (1601), executed for treason. The Bloody Tower, built in the 14thC, contains the room where the 'little princes' are alleged to have been smothered by their uncle, Richard III. The Chapel of St. Peter ad Vincula contains the remains of many of the tower's victims ('no sadder spot on earth' according to the historian Macaulay). The crown jewels are housed in the strongroom beneath the Waterloo Barracks (headquarters of the Royal Fusiliers) and they include St. Edward's Crown, fashioned in gold for the coronation of Charles II (1662) and still used in the ceremony, and the famous Kohinoor diamond (108.8 carats), presented to Queen Victoria in 1850 by the army of the Punjab. See **SIGHTSEEING 2, WALK 3**.

Trafalgar Sq.: London's most famous square was laid out in 1829-41 by Sir Charles Barry. It was intended as a tribute to Horatio Nelson (1758-1805), the distinguished naval commander who died at the Battle of Trafalgar after masterminding a British victory over Napoleon's forces. At the heart of the square, Nelson's Column towers over all. On the north side is the National Gallery (see **ART GALLERIES, A-Z**) with a bronze statue of James II in front. The classical church of St. Martin-in-the-Fields (1721-26), the parish church of the sovereign, stands at the northeast corner (see **CULTURE**). See **SIGHTSEEING 1, WALK 1**.

Victoria, Queen (1819-1901): The first monarch to live in Buckingham Palace (see **A-Z**), Victoria set the tone for the British royal family which continues today. During her 63-year reign London became the centre of the largest empire in the world. After the death in 1861 of her husband and consort, Prince Albert, she commissioned the ornate Albert Memorial in Kensington Gore, but he is probably better remembered by the great South Kensington museums – the Natural History Museum (see **MUSEUMS 1**), the Science Museum (see **MUSEUMS 1**, **A-Z**) and the Victoria and Albert Museum (see **MUSEUMS 1**, **A-Z**), all founded with the proceeds of the Great Exhibition of 1851 which he inspired and organized.

Windsor Castle

Victoria & Albert Museum: The V & A, as it is commonly known, contains a superbly rich and varied collection of exhibits covering the decorative and fine arts, displayed in a maze of galleries containing paintings, ceramics, textiles, carpets, costumes, jewellery, glass and furniture. The exhibits are arranged in Primary Collections according to style, period and nationality, and in special Study Collections by class of object. At least two days are required to appreciate the full wealth of the exhibits, the highlights of which include medieval European and Islamic art, rich Gothic tapestries, arts of Asia, Raphael's Cartoons (1515-16) and English furniture, costumes and domestic designs from earliest times to the 20thC. There are regular lectures and tours on different aspects of the collections. See **MUSEUMS 1**.

West End: London's centre for entertainment and shopping, and the place where most visitors spend much of their time. The area is roughly bounded by Marble Arch, Park Lane and Knightsbridge in the west, and Piccadilly and Soho in the south and east. Within it can be found many of London's most famous shops, world-famous theatres and large cinemas. See **NIGHTLIFE, RESTAURANTS 2, SHOPPING 2, THEATRES**.

Westminster Abbey: Consecrated in 1065 by Edward the Confessor, who is buried behind the altar, the abbey has been the scene of royal coronations for nine centuries, and its very fabric is steeped in English history. The Unknown Warrior, buried just inside the entrance, was brought from France in 1920. The north transept includes graves and memorials to various British statesmen and prime ministers. The royal chapels contain the bones and elaborate tombs of Edward I and III, Richard II, Henry III, V and VII, Elizabeth I, Mary I and many more royals. The wonderful vaulted roof in the Henry VII Chapel is another of the highlights. Poets' Corner includes the tombs of Chaucer, Browning, Tennyson and Spenser, and memorials to many other writers and artists.
Don't miss the cloisters, dating from 1298, and, off them, the Chapterhouse, the Chapel of the Pyx and the Undercroft Museum (combined ticket £1.60, OAP 80p, child 5-15 40p). See **CHURCHES, SIGHTSEEING 1, WALK 1**.

Westminster Abbey

Whitehall: The name of the street that runs between Trafalgar Sq. (see **A-Z**) and the Houses of Parliament (see **Palace of Westminster**). The name of Whitehall is synonymous with 'corridors of power' and the area is the administrative heart of the British government, containing nearly all the major offices of state, including Downing St. Only the Banqueting House, designed by Inigo Jones in Palladian style (1619-22), remains from the original royal Palace of Whitehall, the rest being destroyed by fire in 1698. The main hall has a vast ceiling notable for its nine allegorical paintings by Rubens. In the middle of Whitehall is Horse Guards, the headquarters of the Household Division, who are responsible for the protection of the sovereign. This is the official entrance to the royal palaces and suitably impressive sentries stand guard. Also of interest are the Cabinet Rooms, Winston Churchill's emergency command centre during World War II. See **SIGHTSEEING 1**, **WALK 1**.

Wren, Sir Christopher (1632-1723): Before the arrival of skyscrapers much of the central London skyline was the creation of Christopher Wren. After the Great Fire in 1666 he designed a grid plan of wide streets for London but was thwarted by vested interests and lack of funds. However, between 1670 and 1686 he designed or rebuilt 51 of the City (see **CHURCHES**, **SIGHTSEEING 2**, **WALK 3**, **A-Z**) churches (23 are still intact) while also working on St. Paul's Cathedral (see **CHURCHES**, **SIGHTSEEING 2**, **WALK 3**, **A-Z**), the Royal Hospital (see **Chelsea**), the Monument (see **A-Z**) and the churches of St. Clement Danes (see **WALK 2**) and St. James's, Piccadilly. He also worked on the the royal palaces at Hampton Court (see **EXCURSIONS 1**) and St. James's, and the Old Royal Observatory and the Royal Naval College in Greenwich (see **WALK 4**).

Accidents & Breakdowns: If you are involved in an accident exchange personal particulars and insurance policy details with the other person(s) involved. Contact the police (see **A-Z**) if anyone has been injured or if you suspect drunken driving.

In the event of a breakdown, visitors who are members of motoring organizations in their own countries belonging to the International Touring Alliance can summon help from either the Automobile Association (AA) or the Royal Automobile Club (RAC). Both provide a 24 hr breakdown service which is cheaper than using a garage. They can be summoned using the emergency telephones which are found at regular intervals on motorways. Non-members must pay a surcharge for the use of their services. For more details, contact the AA, Fanum House, Leicester Sq., WC2, tel: 071-8911400 (**U** Leicester Sq.) or the RAC, 89 Pall Mall, SW1, tel: 071-8397050 (**U** Piccadilly Circus). See **Driving**, **Embassies**, **Emergency Numbers**.

Accommodation: Compared with the fairly standardized price/facilities accommodation formula of other countries, accommodation in Britain can vary enormously. If you want to stay in London during the summer you should try to book well in advance (May-Sep. is the busiest period) but if you do arrive with nowhere to stay, the accommodation services of the London Tourist Board (LTB) or British Travel Centre can make arrangements for you (there is a small booking fee). The LTB also produces a useful publication called *Where to Stay in London*. Hotels registered with the LTB are graded by a system of one-five crowns; smaller establishments may be classified as 'listed', normally meaning that facilities are more basic but that they are clean and comfortable. Prices fluctuate considerably according to quality, location and time of year, ranging from £30 to over £400 per night for a room for two people with breakfast. Check that the price you are quoted is inclusive and that hidden extras are not going to creep onto your bill at the end of your stay. Hotel bills include VAT (Value-Added Tax) and service, and usually a 'full English' cooked breakfast (see **Food**). Accommodation is most expensive in the west and southwest of the city where many of the top-quality hotels are located. Modest but comfortable hotels, 'private hotels' and boarding houses can be found around Victoria, Kensington (Earl's Court), Bayswater and Bloomsbury, as well as near the main railway stations (see **Railways**). These vary in quality and price but, being among the most popular types of accommodation, they are usually fully booked in advance of the high season. See **Camping & Caravanning**, **Tourist Information**, **Youth Hostels**.

Airports: Heathrow, the world's busiest airport, is also the closest major airport to London, 16 miles west of the city, adjacent to the M 4. It is linked to the city centre by underground (Piccadilly line) and the journey takes about 50-90 min, depending on the time when you travel. London Transport operates a 24 hr express Airbus to the centre which takes about 60-90 min. Airbus services usually terminate at Victoria coach station although most buses stop at various points in the city. There is also an all-night bus service (N 97) between Heathrow and Trafalgar Sq. A taxi will take about 45 min but can cost over £20. For flight information, tel: 081-7592525.
London's other main airport is Gatwick, 26 miles south of the city, which is linked by rail to Victoria railway station. The Gatwick express operates every 15 min (hourly through the night) and the journey takes about 30 min. There are also regular express-coach services (75 min) to Victoria coach station. A taxi is expensive, at around £20. Gatwick and Heathrow are linked to each other by regular bus services. For flight information, tel: 0293-531299.
The third London airport, Stansted, can be reached by express train (journey time about 40 min) from Liverpool Street railway station. For flight information, tel: 0279-680500.
London's business-orientated City airport is adjacent to King George V Dock, 5 miles east of the city centre (U Plaistow, then taxi). At present it operates scheduled flights to Europe and the Channel Islands; for information, tel: 071-4745555.

Baby-sitters: Most larger hotels operate a baby-listening service. There are also several agencies which provide a baby-sitting or nanny service and will even take children sightseeing. Try Universal Aunts, tel: 071-7388937, or Childminders, tel: 071-9359763. These usually charge an hourly rate plus a registration fee. See CHILDREN, **Children**.

PRIME MERIDIAN
OF THE WORLD

EAST
LONGITUDE

WEST
LONGITUDE

Banks: See **Currency, Money, Opening Times**.

Bicycle & Motorcycle Hire: In theory a good way to see London; in practice quite dangerous due to the heavy traffic and only recommended for those experienced in the hazards of urban cycling or for exploring on a Sun. This applies to bicycles and motorcycles alike. For the latter you will need your driving licence. Many companies only hire to people aged 21 years or over. Rates per day: bicycles from £5; mopeds from £12; motorcycles from £22. Hire companies include the following:

Bike UK Ltd, Lower Robert St, WC2, tel: 071-8392111 (U Covent Garden); Chelsea Bicycles, 13-15 Park Walk, SW10, tel: 071-3523999 (U South Kensington); Portobello Cycles, 69 Golborne Rd, W10; Scootabout, 59 Albert Embankment, SE1, tel: 071-5820055 (BR/U Vauxhall).

Boats: One of the best ways to see London is by motor-launch on the Thames. In summer there are regular services operating between Westminster, Charing Cross and Tower piers, and all service Greenwich Pier. The longest journey – Westminster to Greenwich – takes 45 min and costs £5 return (child £2.50). There are also upstream services from Westminster Pier to Kew (90 min), Richmond (2 hr 30 min) and Hampton Court (3-4 hr).

A relative newcomer to the river is the commuter-oriented Riverbus service. High-speed catamarans ply the waters between Chelsea Harbour, Charing Cross (Hungerford Bridge), Festival Pier (South Bank Centre), Swan Lane Pier (near London Bridge, north bank), London Bridge (south bank), West India Pier (near Marshwall, Docklands) and Greenwich Pier. These operate 0700-2200 Mon.-Fri., 1000-1800 Sat. and Sun.

If you don't mind particularly where you go, there are regular lunchtime and evening cruises with discos, music-hall entertainment and dinner-dances. London Tourist Board's Riverboat Information Service, tel: 071-7304812, gives details of all these cruises.

London's lesser-known waterways are the Regent's and Grand Union canals. They are well worth exploring, either by foot or by taking a gentle cruise on a canal narrowboat. Several companies operate leisure trips along Regent's Canal from Little Venice (the canal area around

Warwick Ave, Westbourne Terr., W9) through Regent's Park to Camden Lock (daily in summer, weekends only in winter). For further information, contact: Jason's Trip, Little Venice, tel: 071-2863428; Jenny Wren, 250 Camden High St, tel: 071-4854433; or London Waterbus Company, Camden Lock, NW1, tel: 071-4822550. Advance booking is advisable.

Budget:

Lunch (snack and drink)	£3-5
Museum ticket	£1.50-3.50
Tea	75p per pot per person
Coffee	£1 per cup
House wine	£8.50 per bottle
Beer	£1.50 per pint

Buses: London Transport's (LT) bus network covers the whole of the city and extends well into the suburbs. The red buses serving the central routes are frequent but are often delayed by heavy traffic and get very crowded during the rush hours. Buses usually run 0630-2400 on most routes and there are a number of all-night services, all of which pass through Trafalgar Sq. Buy your ticket on board from the driver or conductor. As well as single-journey tickets there are various daily and season tickets which allow unlimited travel on all buses; some of these also include travel on train and underground services. Information on bus routes, fares and tickets is listed on a free map which is available from LT information centres (in the following underground stations: Heathrow, King's Cross, Euston, Oxford Circus, Piccadilly Circus, Victoria, Euston) and tourist information centres (see **A-Z**). Alternatively, you can contact London Transport's 24 hr Travel Information Service, tel: 071-2221234.

Green Line Coaches serve the southeast and are ideal for day-trips out of London. The main departure point is Eccleston Bridge near Buckingham Palace Rd, Victoria, SW1. National Express is the main operator for inter-city coach services; ticket and service details can be obtained from the main departure terminal at Victoria coach station, tel: 071-7303499. See **Tours**.

Camping & Caravanning: The nearest site to central London is Tent City, Old Oak Common Lane, Acton, adjacent to Wormwood Scrubs prison. Large, dormitory-style tents are erected with visitors in mind but you can use your own tent if you prefer. Camping is strictly prohibited in London's parks. There are three caravan sites on the outskirts, which also cater for canvas: Abbey Wood Caravan Club, SE2, tel: 081-3102233; Caravan Harbour, Crystal Palace SE19, tel: 081-7787155; and Lee Valley Park, Pickett's Lock, Edmonton, N9, tel: 081-8034756. Expect to pay around £5 per tent per person per night, £6 for caravans. There are also several camp sites on the outskirts of the city and the London Tourist Board (see **Tourist Information**) produces a free list giving details of their locations, costs, facilities and opening times.

Car Hire: Most of the major car-hire companies have offices at the airports and at some railway stations. The minimum-age requirement varies but, generally speaking, you must be over 21 and have held a clean driving licence for at least one year. Expect to pay around £35 per day/£150 per week for a basic car with unlimited mileage, insurance and VAT. The London Tourist Board (see **Tourist Information**) publishes a free list of car-hire companies. See **Driving**.

Chemists: Chemists open during normal shopping hours (0930-1730). Each chemist should carry a notice in the front window indicating the nearest establishment open on a Sun. Boots the Chemist at Piccadilly Circus is open on weekdays until 2000. See **Health**.

Children: For information about children's activities, contact the London Tourist Board's Kidsline, tel: 071-2228070 (1600-1800 Mon.-Fri. term time; 0900-1600 daily, school holidays). Try also to get a copy of the tourist board's excellent publication, *Children's London* (ask at tourist information centres; see **A-Z**). See **CHILDREN**, **Baby-sitters**.

Cinemas: New releases can usually be seen first in West End (see **A-Z**) cinemas, although seats there are more expensive than in their

smaller local counterparts. Some cinema clubs require membership.
Listings magazines (see **What's On**) provide a detailed guide to what is
on offer throughout the city.

More specialized art-house films are shown at places such as as the
Everyman, NW3; the ICA, SW1; the National, South Bank Centre; or
the Screen On The Hill, NW3. Most performances start at 1400 and run
continuously until 2300, although some cinemas show late-night films
from 2300.

Climate: The British climate is nothing if not unpredictable.
However, you should get warm, dry weather (16-21°C) from June-Sep.
and cooler, wet weather at other times of the year. Nov.-Feb. is the
coolest period, with temperatures often dropping to 0°C. It is best to
bring warm clothing and rainwear whatever the season. For weather
information, tel: 071-2468091.

Conversion Chart:

Credit Cards: See **Money**.

Crime & Theft: Take the usual precautions and if you have anything
stolen, report the theft at the nearest police station. When using the
underground (see **A-Z**) beware of pickpockets in crowded places and
do not get into an empty carriage on your own. See **Embassies**,
Emergency Numbers, **Insurance**, **Police**.

Currency: The pound sterling (£) is worth 100 pence (p). Coins in circulation are as follows: 1p and 2p (copper coloured), 5p, 10p, 20p and 50p (silver coloured) and £1 (gold coloured). Notes are £5, £10, £20, £50 and £100. See **Money**.

Customs Allowances:

Duty Free Into:	Cigarettes	or	Cigars	or	Tobacco	Spirits	Wine
EC	300		75		400 g	1.5 l	5 l
UK	300		75		400 g	1.5 l	5 l

Disabled People: Although some museums, theatres and restaurants provide facilities for the disabled, it is always advisable to phone ahead to request assistance and ascertain any particular requirements. The term 'Disabled' which has been used in this book does not denote access to international standards usually implied by the wheelchair symbol but instead is intended to indicate those places which are recommended for wheelchair tourists. The definitive guidebook for disabled visitors to the capital is Nicholson's *Access in London*. Alternatively, call Artsline, the advice service for disabled people in London, on 071-3882227/8, 1000-1600 Mon.-Fri., 1000-1400 Sat.

Drinks: Beer is the traditional British alcoholic drink and although it is a generic term including lager, it generally refers to bitter, a brownish-coloured brew which should be served cool but never chilled. There are hundreds of variations in taste, body and strength so try to specify a particular brand. If you're not sure, ask for a pint or a half of ordinary or strong bitter or lager. Lager is almost as popular as bitter in

Britain but you will find it a poor and weak imitation of its European namesake. You won't have to ask for 'real ale' (natural cask-conditioned beer) as almost every pub serves it. Wines from all over the world are readily available, including some excellent British varieties but these generally cost a little more. As well as soft drinks there are some good low- and non-alcohol beers and lagers available in every good pub, so never be tempted to drink and drive.

Tea is the other great British drink and afternoon tea ('high tea' is an archaic term) is one of the few remaining quintessential English pastimes. See PUBS, Pubs.

Driving: You can drive in Britain with an international driving permit or a driving licence from your country of origin. The minimum age for driving a car is 17. Drive on the left and overtake on the right. The speed limit in residential areas is 30 mph (48 kph), 60 mph (96 kph) on dual carriageways and 70 mph (112 kph) on motorways. All road regulations are explained in the *Highway Code* (available at most bookshops and newsagents, £1). The driver and passenger must always wear seat belts in the front and back (if the car is fitted with rear seat belts). You must also use a child restraint if you are carrying a child less than a year old in the front seat.

Visitors should not drive in London unless absolutely necessary, as conditions are generally chaotic – latest figures show that traffic moves at an average speed of 8 mph (13 kph) and that the congestion is getting worse. In addition, the capital's roads were not designed for motor traffic and their layout can be confusing. If you do decide to drive, a road map which shows one-way streets is essential. See **Accidents & Breakdowns**, **Car Hire**, **Parking**, **Petrol**.

Drugs: All drugs are illegal and there are severe penalties for offenders. If you are a foreigner and are arrested for a drugs-related offence, contact your embassy (see **A-Z**).

Eating Out: London offers a vast range of tempting cuisines from all over the world. There are large numbers of restaurants around Covent

Garden (see **A-Z**), the West End (see **A-Z**) and South Kensington (see **Kensington**), while Soho (see **A-Z**) in particular offers an exotic variety of eating places at reasonable prices and is famous for its Chinatown restaurants. For more informal meals, there are many fast-food outlets. Many department stores too, have reasonably priced eating places, and while most pubs and wine bars serve food at lunchtime, the quality is very variable. There is no official classification for eating places but specialist publications by Egon Ronay, *Which?* (Consumers' Association) and *Time Out* (see **What's On**) provide expert guidance to the best, and the worst, on offer. Price categories in the RESTAURANTS pages are based on a mid-price, à la carte, three-course meal for one with coffee but excluding wine, and are as follows: Inexpensive – under £10; Moderate – £10-15; Expensive – £15-25. See RESTAURANTS 1-3, **Food**.

Electricity: 220-240 V AC. Visitors from overseas bringing their own electrical appliances may need an adaptor (available from airport shops and electrical-goods retailers).

Embassies:
Republic of Ireland – 17 Grosvenor Pl., SW1, tel: 071-2352171
Australia – Australia House, The Strand, WC2, tel: 071-4388000
Canada – Canadian High Commission, Macdonald House, 1 Grosvenor Sq., W1, tel: 071-6299492
New Zealand – 80 Haymarket, SW1, tel: 071-9308422
USA – 24 Grosvenor Sq., W1, tel: 071-4999000

Emergency Numbers: Tel: 999 (free) for police, fire brigade or ambulance.

Events:
1 January: Lord Mayor of Westminster's Parade; *First fortnight in January:* International Boat Show, Earl's Court Exhibition Centre. *Late January/early February:* Chinese New Year, with festivities and parades around Leicester Sq. and Soho.

Late March/early April: Oxford v Cambridge University Boat Race from Putney to Mortlake; *Easter Sunday:* Easter Parade, Battersea Park; *Easter Monday:* London Harness Horse Parade, Inner Circle, Regent's Park.

21 April (or Monday following if on Sunday): Queen's Birthday, with gun salutes from Hyde Park and the Tower; *23 (St. George's Day):* Shakespeare's Birthday Service, Southwark Cathedral; *Late April:* London Marathon (Europe's largest), from Blackheath/Greenwich to Westminster Bridge.

May: Chelsea Flower Show, Royal Hospital, Chelsea; *Second Sunday:* Punch-and-Judy Festival, Covent Garden Piazza.

Second Saturday in June: The Queen's (official) Birthday Parade – Trooping the Colour, Horse Guards Parade; *Last week in June & first week in July:* Wimbledon Lawn Tennis Championships.

July: City of London Festival, with arts events at various venues; Royal Tournament, a pageant staged by the British armed forces, Earl's Court; Dogget's Coat and Badge Race, 275-year-old single-sculls race from London Bridge to Chelsea; *Mid-July (continuing to mid-September):* Sir Henry Wood Promenade Concerts (Proms), Royal Albert Hall.

August, Bank Holiday Sunday and Monday: Notting Hill Carnival, Notting Hill/Ladbroke Grove.

15 September: Battle of Britain Day, with a fly past of aircraft over the city.

First Sunday in October: Pearly Kings and Queens Harvest Festival service, St. Martin-in-the-Fields; *Nearest Sunday to 21st:* Trafalgar Day parade and service, Trafalgar Sq.

First Sunday in November: London to Brighton Veteran Car Run, starting from Hyde Park; *Second Saturday:* Lord Mayor's Show (see **City**); *Sunday nearest 11th:* Remembrance Day Service, Cenotaph, Whitehall; *Mid-November:* State Opening of Parliament by the queen; Christmas illuminations turned on in Regent St and Oxford St.

Early December: Trafalgar Sq. Christmas tree erected; *26-28:* Carol services in Westminster Abbey, St. Paul's, Southwark Cathedral and Trafalgar Sq.; *31:* Midnight New Year celebrations in Trafalgar Sq.

A free diary of London events and entertainments can be obtained from tourist information centres (see **A-Z**), or tel: 071-2468041.

Guides: London Blue Badge guides have passed examinations set by the London Tourist Board and are the only guides employed by reputable tour operators, travel agents and sightseeing tour companies. The Driver Guides' Association, tel: 081-6744802, and Professional Guide Services, tel: 081-8742745, both provide Blue Badge guides who will give tours tailored to your requirements. Charges range from £100-280 depending on whether the tour is a half or full day. Walking tours are an excellent way of seeing the parts of London that the coach tours cannot reach and, at around £4 for 2 hr, they are unbeatable value. There are several walking-tour companies but the best is The Original London Walks, tel: 071-4356413. See **Tours**.

Health: Free medical treatment and subsidized dental care for short-term foreign visitors is available to EC nationals and the citizens of other countries with reciprocal arrangements (including Australia and New Zealand but not the USA). You can consult a National Health Service (NHS) doctor or dentist but you will have to pay, so it is essential that you take out health insurance before leaving home. The following hospitals have 24 hr casualty departments in case of emergencies (accident and emergency patients are not charged): St. Bartholomew's Hospital, West Smithfield, EC1, tel: 071-6018888; U St. Paul's; Charing Cross Hospital, Fulham Palace Rd, SW6, tel: 081-8461234; U Hammersmith Broadway; St. Thomas's Hospital, Lambeth Palace Rd, SE1, tel: 071-9289292; U Westminster; University College, Gower St, WC1, tel: 071-3879300; U Warren St; Moorfields Eye Hospital, High Holborn, WC1, tel: 071-2533411; U Holborn. See **Chemists**, **Disabled People**, **Emergency Numbers**, **Insurance**.

Insurance: Travel insurance should cover you against theft and loss of property and money, as well as medical expenses. See **Crime & Theft**, **Driving**, **Health**.

Laundries: Larger hotels have their own facilities. Launderettes offer same-day service washes costing about £2.50 and most are open every day. Names and addresses of laundries can be found in the local *Yellow Pages* or in the business volume of the telephone directory.

Lost Property Offices:

General losses – enquire at the police station nearest to where the loss occurred or at the Metropolitan Police Lost Property Office, 15 Penton St, W1 (0900-1600 Mon.-Fri. No telephone enquiries).
British Rail – ask at the lost property office of the relevant station.
London Transport Bus and Underground – Enquiries to 200 Baker St, W1 (0930-1730 Mon.-Fri. No telephone enquiries).
Taxis – Metropolitan Police Lost Property Office, 15 Penton St, W1.
Airlines – contact the relevant carrier. If the loss occurred inside the airport buildings, contact the airport police.

Money: Sterling traveller's cheques are accepted in most major stores, but they usually charge a commission and you will get a better rate of exchange at banks. Remember to take your passport as proof of identity when changing money. The bureaux de change in the main railway stations (Victoria, Charing Cross and Waterloo) are open late. Beware of the high commission charged by some of the bureaux de change – look for an LTB-registered sign and ask the rate before you change any money. Major credit cards are widely accepted, although some stores, such as Fortnum & Mason, John Lewis and Marks & Spencer, only accept their own cards or cheques accompanied by a banker's card. See **Crime & Theft**, **Currency**.

Newspapers: See **What's On**.

Nightlife: London's West End (see **A-Z**) is the theatre capital of the world (see **THEATRES**, **Theatres**) and also provides film fans with a wide choice of cinemas showing everything from popular releases to art-house movies (see **Cinemas**). The Royal Opera House, Coliseum and Sadler's Wells Theatre offer a feast of delights for lovers of opera and ballet, and there is a regular programme of music concerts and recitals at the Royal Festival Hall, Barbican Centre and South Bank Centre (see **CULTURE**). For those who just fancy a night out on the town there are numerous pubs, wine bars, nightclubs, discos, cabarets, alternative-comedy clubs, and rock, pop and jazz venues to suit all tastes and budgets (see **MUSIC VENUES**, **NIGHTLIFE**, **PUBS**). See **What's On**.

Opening Times:
Banks – 0930-1500/1530 Mon.-Fri. Some main branches open
0930-1200 Sat.
Post offices – 0900-1730 Mon.-Fri., 0900-1230 Sat. Smaller offices in
the suburbs may close at lunchtime.
Pubs – traditional hours: 1100-1430/1500, 1730-2300 Mon.-Sat., 1200-
1400, 1900-2230 Sun.; all-day opening: 1100-2300 Mon.-Sat., 1200-
1500, 1900-2230 Sun.
Shops – 0900/0930-1730 Mon.-Sat. Some larger stores open until 1900
or 2000 on Wed. or Thu. In the City (see **A-Z**) most shops are closed
on Sat.

Parking: Parking is very difficult in all central London areas. On-
street parking is mostly regulated by parking meters which take 10p,
20p, 50p and £1 coins, usually for a maximum of 2 hr (0830-1830
Mon.-Fri., 0830-1330 or 1830 Sat.). There is no charge on Sun. or Sat.
afternoons in some districts.
For sightseeing it is best to park in an outer London area and then travel
into the centre by public transport. However, if you want to park nearer
to the centre, Hyde Park multistorey car park has one of the best locations of any of the central car parks but to get there you have to drive
through heavy traffic then pay a hefty parking fee.
If you park illegally you will get a parking ticket, and if your car is
judged to be causing an obstruction it will be impounded or wheel-
clamped by the police and you will have to go to the nearest police station to pay a fine and have the car released. See **Driving**.

Passports & Customs: You will need your passport but not a visa
unless you intend staying longer than six months. There is no limit on
the amount of money you can bring into or out of the country. For visitors from the EC, the normal community customs regulations apply. See
Customs Allowances.

Petrol: This is expensive, costing around 48p per litre. Unleaded is
around 2p per litre cheaper. Petrol stations (usually self-service) are
quite common. See **Driving**.

Police: You will still see the British 'bobby', dressed in dark blue uniform and distinctive helmet, walking the beat. The Metropolitan Police wear blue-and-white armbands; their headquarters are at the corner of Broadway and Victoria St, SW1, tel: 071-2301212. The City (see **A-Z**) Police wear distinctive helmets and red-and-white armbands; their head office is at 37 Wood St, EC2, tel: 071-6012222. See **Crime & Theft**, **Emergency Numbers**.

Post Offices: The London chief post office is at 24 William IV St, WC2 (0800-2000 Mon. & Wed.-Sat., 0830-2200 Tue. BR/U Charing Cross). Stamps are also on sale at newsagents and other outlets. A first-class stamp costs 24p and will almost guarantee next-day delivery to a UK mainland address. Second-class postage costs 19p but delivery the next day is fairly unlikely. Letters marked 'poste restante' and addressed to the chief post office (see above) will be kept for a fortnight. Proof of identity is required before they will be released.

Public Holidays: These are also known as bank holidays (BH) and banks, post offices and public buildings close. Most shops and attractions stay open. Pubs usually open Sun. hours (see **Opening Times**). New Year's Day (1 Jan.); Good Fri.; Easter Mon.; May Day (first Mon. in May); Spring BH (last Mon. in May); Summer BH (last Mon. in Aug.); Christmas Day (25 Dec.); Boxing Day (26 Dec.). If a fixed-date holiday falls on a weekend, the following Mon. becomes a holiday.

Railways: Britain's railway system is a nationalized industry run by British Rail (BR) and though much maligned, gets most of the people to the right place most of the time. Expect delays at the weekends due to engineering works.
Trains are split into first- and second-class compartments and unless you specify what you want when buying your ticket you will be sold a second-class one which is usually adequate for a short journey outside rush hour. A first-class ticket will cost you up to 50% more except at weekends when only a small supplement is charged (subject to 'weekend first-class' carriage availability). It is advisable to book a seat in advance whenever possible. Children 5-15 travel half-price but OAPs

must buy a Railcard to qualify for discounts. The choice of tickets, depending on your destination and timing, is often quite baffling, so tell the BR ticket office your timing options and let them advise you on the best deal. Tickets can be purchased to cover transfers to the underground, and the main railway stations are linked by both underground and bus. Bus Link connects Waterloo with Euston, St. Pancras and King's Cross stations. Red Arrow buses also link Waterloo and Liverpool St stations (Bus 502) and Waterloo and Victoria stations (Bus 507). London's main stations serve the following regions:

Charing Cross – Southern Region; London Bridge – Southern Region; Fenchurch St – Eastern Region, including Docklands; Marylebone – Western Region; Waterloo – Southern Region for services to the west of England; Euston – north Midlands, north Wales, northwest England and west of Scotland; King's Cross – east and northeast England and east of Scotland; Liverpool St – East Anglia and Essex; Paddington – west and southwest England, south Midlands and south Wales; St. Pancras – north Midlands; Victoria – south and southeast England and Gatwick. Generally speaking, suburban trains run 0600-2400 Mon.-Sat., 0700-2330 Sun. Times and details of services are available from local stations, from BR Travel Centres at the main stations, where you can also buy rail tickets and make advance reservations, or from the British Travel Centre, 12 Regent St, SW1, tel: 071-7303400 (0900-1830 Mon.-Fri., 1000-1600 Sat. & Sun.; later in summer. U Piccadilly Circus). For details of the Docklands Light Railway, see **Docklands**.

Religious Services: City (see **A-Z**) churches hold midday services during the week but are often closed on Sun.

Church of England – St. Paul's Cathedral, EC4; Westminster Abbey, SW1; Southwark Cathedral, SE1; St. Martin-in-the-Fields, Trafalgar Sq., WC2.

Catholic – Westminster Cathedral, Ashley Pl., Victoria St, SW1; Brompton Oratory, Brompton Rd, SW7; St. George's Cathedral, Lambeth, SE1; Church of the Immaculate Conception, Farm St, Berkeley Sq., W1.

Jewish – West London Synagogue, 34 Upper Berkeley St, W1; Central Synagogue, Great Portland St, W1.

Baptist – Bloomsbury Central, Shaftesbury Ave (New Oxford St), W1.
Methodist – Central Hall, Westminster, SW1.
Society of Friends (Quaker) – Friends' House, Euston Rd, NW1.
Church of Scotland – St. Columba's, Pont St, SW1.
Greek Orthodox – 184 Mare St, E8.
Islam – The Mosque, Regent's Park, NW1.

Shopping: London is a shopper's paradise, offering a bewildering choice, from world-famous stores to unique specialist shops. If you think big is best, head for Oxford St, with its array of department stores, but for specialist shopping on a more intimate scale, try Covent Garden (see **A-Z**). Fashion shoppers should make for the exclusive jewellers and designer boutiques of Regent St, Bond St and Piccadilly (see **A-Z**).

Savile Row is famous for its tailors; Tottenham Court Rd is packed with furniture, electrical and hi-fi shops, and the second-hand book shops around Charing Cross are a mecca for bibliophiles. Non-EC visitors to Britain may be able to obtain VAT (Value-Added Tax) refunds: get a form from the shop from which you make your purchase, fill it in and have it stamped by the assistant. When you leave the country, hand the form to customs staff at the airport and expect to wait for around six weeks for a refund. See **MARKETS**, **SHOPPING 1 & 2**, **Opening Times**.

Smoking: Smoking is not permitted in any part of the underground, or on buses. Trains have separate clearly-marked smoking carriages. Increasingly, no smoking is becoming the rule in all public places.

Sports: Participatory sports:
Golf – Courses open to non-members are at Ealing, tel: 081-9970937; Ruislip, tel: 0895-638835; and Richmond Park, tel: 081-8763205. Green fees £10-20, club hire £5-8 per half set.
Riding – Belmont Riding Centre, NW7, tel: 081-9591588; Ross Nye, W2 – who ride in Hyde Park, tel: 071-2623791; Wimbledon Village Stables SW19, tel: 081-9468579. Private tuition £20 per hr.
Ice-skating – Broadgate Ice Rink, EC2, tel: 071-5886565; Queen's Ice-skating Club, Queensway, W2. £3 per session exclusive of skate hire.
Tennis – There are public tennis courts at the following parks: Battersea Park; Holland Park; Hyde Park; Lincoln's Inn Fields; Parliament Hill (Hampstead Heath); and Regent's Park. £3-4 per hr.
Spectator sports:
Athletics – Crystal Palace National Sports Centre (mostly summer), tel: 081-7780131.
Cricket – Lord's Cricket Ground, St. John's Wood Rd, NW8. That most English of sports is probably best sampled at Lord's on a summer Sun. afternoon. There is a museum and tours which may help to explain the mysteries of the game; tel: 071-2663825 for details.
Football – Wembley Stadium is the home ground of the England football team and the venue of the FA Cup final. There are organized tours around the ground and behind the scenes on most days. In Aug. it hosts the American Football Bowl, tel: 081-9028833. For first-division

English league football, try Arsenal, tel: 071-2260304; Chelsea, tel: 071-3816221; Tottenham Hotspur, tel: 081-8013323. Seats £8-15. Horse racing – the nearest major racecourse is Kempton Park, Sunbury-on-Thames (near Hampton Court); tel: 09327-82292.

Tennis – All-England Tennis Club, Church Rd, Wimbledon, SW19. The last week of June and first week of July is the time for strawberries and cream and, of course, the Wimbledon All-England Championships. The main building also houses the Lawn Tennis Museum (1100-1700 Mon.-Sat., 1400-1700 Sun.; £1.50, OAP/child 5-16 75p). The Queen's Club, Barons Court, hosts the annual Stella Artois pre-Wimbledon tournament; tel: 071-3853421.

Wembley Arena (adjacent to Wembley Stadium) hosts showjumping, tennis, boxing and other major sporting events. Another sport associated with everyday London life is greyhound racing which takes place at Catford, Hackney, Wimbledon, Haringay, Walthamstow and Wembley; the *Evening Standard* (see **What's On**) has details.

Taxis: Look out for the famous black taxi cabs (which may also be purple, red or other colours!). The rear licence plate will tell you they are a registered 'hackney carriage' and they can be hailed if the yellow 'for hire' sign is lit. You can also hire from taxi ranks (outside the major stations) or by telephone. There is a fixed charge on the meter (minimum £1, plus 20p per person) to which further charges are added depending on the distance covered. Ask what the approximate cost will be if travelling long distances. Additional charges are levied for luggage carried beside the driver, and if the journey begins or ends between 2400-0600, or on a Sun. or a public holiday (see **A-Z**). It is customary to give a 10% tip (see **Tipping**). Any other form of taxi is known as a minicab. These are generally not metered and you should establish the fare before setting off. They can be cheaper than metered cabs over longer distances but they cannot be hailed on the street and should be avoided if they are touting for trade as this is illegal.

Telephones & Telegrams: Public telephones can be found in most streets, railway stations, pubs, hotels and restaurants. The traditional red box, however, has given way in most places to a smoked-glass cubicle. Payphones accept 10p, 20p, 50p and £1 coins. Booths contain dialling instructions and coins not used are refunded when the receiver is replaced, so it's best to insert lots of smaller coins.

Cardphones are indicated by a green sign. The minimum cost is £1 for a 10-unit card which is obtainable from post offices, tobacconists and shops displaying the green cardphone sticker. If you intend calling abroad, buy a 40- or 100-unit card.

International calls can be made direct from any telephone by dialling the country code, followed by the area code and then the number required. Country codes are as follows:

Republic of Ireland	tel: 010-353	Australia	tel: 010-61
Canada	tel: 010-1	USA	tel: 010-1
New Zealand	tel: 010-64		

The following numbers may also be useful:

Directory enquiries (dialling in London)	tel: 142
(dialling outside London)	tel: 192
Operator	tel: 100
International operator	tel: 155
International directory enquiries	tel: 153

Telemessages have replaced telegrams in the UK and this 24 hr service is available by dialling the telemessage operator, tel: 190. Telemessages should arrive on the following working day but they can take longer. An international telemessage service is available to the USA only.

British Telecom's International Communications Centre at 1a Broadway, SW1, tel: 071-2224444 (0900-2000) has facilities for sending telegrams and telexes, and making international calls. A similar facility is available at Heathrow airport terminals 3 and 4.

Television & Radio: ITV London is shared by Thames TV and London Weekend Television (LWT), and features news, popular entertainment, sport and films. Don't expect a TV in your hotel room unless it has been specified.

Local radio stations are as follows: LBC on 261 m/1152 kHz or 97.3 mHz (with news and events coverage); Capital Radio on 194 m/1548 kHz or 95.8 mHz (featuring news, current affairs, pop and ethnic material); Greater London Radio (GLR) on 94.9 mHz (broadcasting news, current affairs and pop music). There are BBC local stations serving the London area, as well as the five national stations.

Theatres: In addition to information in the *Evening Standard* and the listings magazines (see **What's On**), the Society of West End Theatres (SWET) produces a free fortnightly theatre guide which is available at hotels, booking offices and tourist information centres (see **A-Z**). Tickets can be purchased at the box office or by phone using a credit card. Theatre booking agents charge a commission but can often get seats for shows which are otherwise sold out. Students can get standby tickets at reduced prices just before curtain-up. The SWET ticket booth in Leicester Sq. sells cheap tickets for available performances on the same day (1200-1400 for matinees, 1430-1830 for evening performances) and adds a small commission charge. Some fringe theatres and clubs require membership but visitors can join before the show for a nominal fee. See **THEATRES**.

Tipping: It is generally accepted that you should tip taxi drivers, restaurant staff and hairdressers around 10% if you are happy with their service. Hotel chambermaids, luggage porters and tour guides also are tipped. Some restaurants automatically add a service charge onto your bill. If you feel the service didn't warrant the charge, you are within your rights to refuse to pay it but you will have to tell the manager your reasons. Pub bar staff are never tipped but if you want to show appreciation, ask if they would like a drink, which they may accept in liquid or cash form!

Toilets: You will find these in department stores (often the best-kept), train and bus stations (main stations have 'super loos' with showers, shaving sockets and baby-changing facilities), main streets (often in the worst state) and pubs and restaurants which you shouldn't use unless you are a patron. Coin-operated toilets can be found in several central locations, including Leicester Sq., Victoria St and Soho.

Tourist Information: The London Tourist Board (LTB) offers a good service and provides free maps and leaflets plus an on-the-spot hotel-booking service. They will sell you theatre, excursion and travel tickets, and provide a list of official blue-badge, LTB-trained guides (see **A-Z**). They also deal with complaints (which must be made in writing). Their main tourist information centre is at Victoria station forecourt, SW1 (0800-1900 Mon.-Sat., 0800-1700 Sun.; later in summer). Other main tourist information centres are at:

Harrods, Knightsbridge, SW1 (basement banking hall, open store hours. U Knightsbridge); Selfridges, Oxford St, W1 (basement service arcade, open store hours Easter-Oct.; 1030-1800 Mon.-Sat., 0930-2000 Thu., Nov.-Easter. U Marble Arch, Bond St); Heathrow Airport, Terminals 1, 2, 3 underground station (concourse, 0800-1830 daily); Liverpool St underground station, EC2 (0930-1830 Mon.-Fri., 0830-1830 Sat., 0830-1530 Sun.); Tower of London, West Gate, EC3 (0930-1800 Mon.-Sat., 1000-1800 Sun., Easter-Nov.). There are also several other tourist information centres in the London boroughs, including Greenwich and Richmond.

Other organizations which give information and are of use to visitors to the city include the following:

City of London Information Centre, St. Paul's Churchyard, EC4 (0930-1700 Mon.-Sat. Closes 1230 Sat., Nov.-April. U St. Paul's); and the British Travel Centre, 12 Regent St, SW1, tel: 071-7303400 (0900-1830 Mon.-Fri., 1000-1600 Sat. & Sun. U Piccadilly Circus). The British Travel Centre combines the British Tourist Authority and British Rail (you can buy rail tickets and reserve seats; see **Railways**). It has multi-lingual staff who provide a booking service for theatre and tour tickets, an accommodation service and a bureau de change. If you would like some information before you leave home, write to LTB Head Office, 26 Grosvenor Gardens, London SW1, tel: 071-7303450.

Tours: The best way to see London is from the top of a double-decker bus. London Transport (LT) runs The Original Sightseeing Tour which departs regularly from Victoria, Marble Arch, Haymarket and Baker St underground station. The commentary is live and an open-top bus is used in summer (1 hr 30 min; £8, child 5-15 £4, tel: 071-2273456). LT also runs other coach tours on weekdays throughout the year, with prices ranging from £10.50 to £39. Coaches depart from Wilton Rd coach station (near Victoria). Tickets can be bought on board and reservations and further information can be obtained from LT (see **Buses**) or tourist information centres (see **A-Z**). See **Guides**.

Transport: The quickest way of travelling around is by underground. Taxis are more convenient for complicated routes, but are fairly expensive. The best way to see London, however, is on foot (see **Guides**) or by bus (see **Tours**). The capital's waterways are not the major thoroughfares they once were but ferries still operate on the Thames from various piers. London is ringed with main-line railway stations with services to almost every part of Britain, and is also served by three international airports.

Many types of saver ticket are available which combine bus, train and underground travel; ask for details at a London Transport or tourist information centre (see **A-Z**). See **Airports**, **Boats**, **Buses**, **Railways**, **Taxis**, **Underground**.

Traveller's Cheques: See **Money**.

Underground: The underground, or 'tube' as it is commonly known, is the fastest and easiest way to travel around the city. Services run 0530-2400 Mon.-Sat., 0700-2400 Sun. and are crammed full in rush hours (0800-0930/1700-1830). In central London you are never more than a few minutes' walk away from a station. Maps in the stations will show which is the most direct route to your destination. There are six fare zones and the cost increases the more zones you travel through. Buy your ticket from the ticket office or adjacent machines before you begin your journey and keep it for collection at your destination. Five-16-year-olds travel at a reduced rate; 14-16-year-olds should obtain a Child Rate Photocard (available free at post offices and underground stations). Under 5s travel free. See **Crime & Theft**.

What's On: The *Evening Standard* is London's only evening newspaper and it provides reasonable coverage of local news and events. For more detailed events news, see the weekly listings magazines. The best of these is *Time Out*, though this is designed more for Londoners than for tourists and is not so immediately accessible as *What's On & Where to Go*. Look out too for *City Limits*. Most newspaper stands in central London sell American and Continental newspapers, and an extensive range of foreign papers can be found in the following newsagents: 118 Fleet St, EC2; 104-06 Long Acre, WC2; and 48 Old Compton St, W1.

Youth Hostels: You have to be a member of the Youth Hostel Association (YHA) before you can use any of the London hostels. The best is in the grounds of the Commonwealth Institute, Holland Park, Kensington, W8, tel: 071-9370748. There are others at: 84 Highgate West Hill, N6, tel: 081-3401831; 38 Bolton Gardens, Earl's Court, SW5, tel: 071-3737083; and 4 Wellgarth Rd, Hampstead Heath, NW11, tel: 081-4589054. For more details, contact the YHA, 14 Southampton St, WC2, tel: 071-2403158, or any tourist information centre (see **A-Z**). Expect to pay somewhere around £9-12 per night.

This book was produced using QuarkXPress™
and Adobe Illustrator 88™ on Apple
Macintosh™ computers and output to separated·
film on a Linotronic 300 Imagesetter

Text: Elizabeth Claridge & Paul Murphy
Photography: Michael Dent
& Phil Springthorpe (28)
Electronic Cartography: Compo Rive Gauche

First published 1990
Second Edition 1992
Copyright © HarperCollins Publishers
Published by HarperCollins Publishers
Printed by HarperCollins Manufacturing,
Glasgow
ISBN 0 00 470019-8